Praise for Bobby Deen's *From Mama's Table to Mine*

"Bobby Deen nails it with these favorite Southern recipes. What they've lost in calories, they've gained in flavor. Perfect for everything from a quick weeknight meal to an elaborate Saturday-night celebration."

—Rocco DiSpirito, chef and author

"It's so great that Bobby has refashioned some all-time favorite Southern dishes in a healthier style. He continues to work hard to keep America healthy and happy."

—Curtis Stone, chef, television host, and author

"Thanks, Bobby Deen, for giving us 120 delicious reasons why we can have our cake and eat it too . . . quickly! From Hush Puppies, to Slow-Cooked North Carolina–Style Pulled Pork, to one of my favorite childhood sandwiches, the Crispy, Crunchy Reuben, to a number of delicious desserts, all the bases are covered. If you love Southern food—without the calories or the time commitment—you'll want this cookbook!"

—Carla Hall, host of ABC's *The Chew*

"Bobby Deen has been our 'brother from another mother,' and when you taste his dishes, you immediately recognize Paula's influence. His tasty food stresses eating healthier without sacrificing the delicious Southern flavors and traditions he grew up with! Way to go, Bobby!"

—Pat and Gina Neely, hosts of *Down Home with the Neelys*

By Jamie and Bobby Deen and Melissa Clark

THE DEEN BROS. GET FIRED UP

THE DEEN BROS. TAKE IT EASY

THE DEEN BROS. COOKBOOK: RECIPES FROM THE ROAD

THE DEEN BROS.: Y'ALL COME EAT

From Mama's Table to Mine

BOBBY DEEN

AND MELISSA CLARK

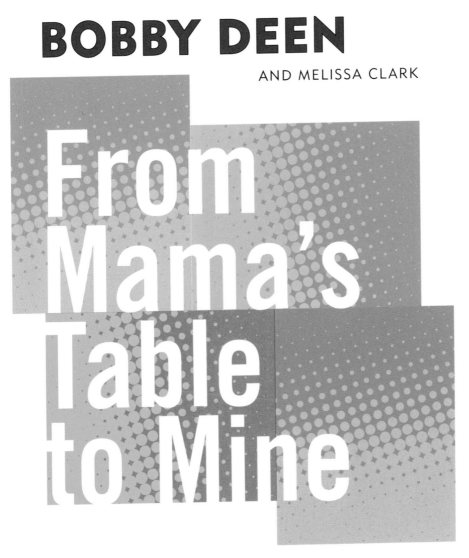

From Mama's Table to Mine

Everybody's Favorite Comfort Foods
at **350 CALORIES OR LESS**

BALLANTINE BOOKS TRADE PAPERBACKS · NEW YORK

Published in the United States by Ballantine Books, an imprint of
The Random House Publishing Group, a division of Random House, Inc., New York.

BALLANTINE and colophon are registered trademarks of Random House, Inc.

LIBRARY OF CONGRESS CATALOGING-IN-PUBLICATION DATA
Deen, Bobby.
From Mama's table to mine : everybody's favorite comfort foods at 350
calories or less / Bobby Deen and Melissa Clark.
pages   cm.
Includes index.
ISBN 978-0-345-53663-1 (pbk.) — ISBN 978-0-345-53665-5 (ebook) 1.
Low-calorie diet—Recipes. 2. Comfort food. I. Clark, Melissa. II.
Title.
RM222.2.D443 2012
641.5'63—dc23   2012033950

Printed in the United States of America

www.ballantinebooks.com

9 8 7 6 5 4 3 2 1

Book design by Liz Cosgrove

Mama, this book is dedicated to you. You taught me everything I know about making food that makes people happy. Your unconditional love and support continues to be the guiding force in my life. With you in my corner, I know the sky's the limit. I love you.

Contents

Introduction

DOWN HERE IN GEORGIA, we're fond of that old saying "Eat like a champ." When we see someone really digging into food and enjoying it, we're sure to proudly clap him on the back and congratulate him. Well, I reckon that saying certainly applies to me. Of course I know how to eat like a champ; I've been taught by the best, y'all, Paula Deen. I love my Mama's food, it truly is the best-tasting food on this planet. But, let's face it. I can't eat her rich food every day of my life. While I was lucky enough to be raised on Mama's dishes, there came a day when I had to find a way to dial it back a bit. And being the champion eater that I am, I was determined to find a way to slim down my favorite recipes without losing one ounce of flavor.

The way I see it, eating right and living healthier is not about sacrifice, it's about making good choices that keep you satisfied. For that understanding I have to give credit to the second most important influence in my life, my coach and good friend Sam Carter. Sam and I met when I was thirty years old, but I looked and felt like I was at least ten years older. He made me realize that being healthy is much more than just showing up at the gym. Being healthy is a whole lifestyle and mind-set. And that thinking has made all the difference in helping me look and feel younger. No matter where I am in my life, Sam's words of wisdom stay with me.

Even though my work and personal lives are busy and often take me far from Savannah, I try to make it to my Mama's place for Sunday dinner as often as I can. There's just nothing like sitting round her great-big-old kitchen table with the whole family gathered to share in her amazing food. Mama doesn't end up eating too much at these gatherings because she's so busy feeding us, but we all manage to get in a hearty feast.

From my **Chicken-Fried Steak with Cream Gravy** (page 71) to **Yes You Can Mac and Cheese** (page 102), right on down to **Red Velvet Cake** (page 168), these are the types of foods that I looked forward to as a boy. And you'll find them all right here, along with dozens more mouthwatering comfort foods. What you won't find are the heavy calories and fat you'd expect, because I've lightened them all up, as you can see from the before and after calories and fat info I've included with each recipe. I like to call this process turning Sunday food into Monday food. Who wants to wait all week to enjoy these tasty treats? I certainly do not. But I know that I can't load myself up with the calories these dishes usually contain. So I sat down, took a good look at these favorite recipes, found the major culprits in them, and took the fat and calories down a notch without losing any of their great flavor and appeal. I came up with 120 comforting, down-home recipes, all containing 350 calories or fewer per serving. Then I shared them with my Mama. I knew I was on to something when she proclaimed, "Sonny boy, are you sure you remembered to take down the fat and calories? Because I still taste all the great flavor I'd expect in these down-home classics."

You see, I still want good food on the table, even when that food is good for me. And I also like it to be quick. I'm sure you're as busy as I am, so I think you're going to like the fact that these recipes make fast and easy meals. Take a dish like **Rotelle Pasta Salad with Garlicky Broccoli and Mozzarella** (page 50). Grill a piece of chicken or fish and set it alongside this quick make-ahead salad and you've got yourself an almost-instant meal. Or whip up **The Son's Beef Vegetable Soup** (page 31), tack on a side salad, and you've got yourself a hearty lunch or light but satisfying dinner.

Because eating right is an all-day affair, I've included some of my favorite breakfast recipes too. I wasn't always sold on breakfast, but nowadays, I make sure I get something into my body to fuel me up for the day. Whether it is something as quick and simple as a **Toasted-Waffle Ham and Egg Sandwich** (page 158) or a dish that's just a little more decadent like **Pecan Waffles with Strawberry Syrup** (page 160), these recipes have the nutrients to get me going.

In the middle of the day, armed with my fast and fresh sandwich, soup, and salad recipes, you'll find it's easier to make the right food choices. Soups, especially, are great to have around the house. I cook up a big batch of **The Son's Chicken Noodle Soup** (page 24) so that I have plenty in the fridge or freezer for a quick lunch. And that's really helpful on days when I'm hungry and rushed and would be tempted to turn to fast food.

In the end, my healthy lifestyle is all about balance: between exercise, downtime, healthy food, and even splurges. I've shared some of the best tips that help me maintain a balanced life. Keep an eye out for exercise tips, smart serving suggestions, and some nifty chef's secrets scattered throughout the book. Plus, there's a special bonus chapter in the back containing a week of fifteen-hundred-calories-a-day menus; healthy activities and tips; party menus; tips for stocking the pantry, fridge, and freezer; and a helpful list of healthy lower-fat subs and swaps.

I guess this book is a little bit of a love letter to my Mama and my Mama's people before her. It's nice to know I don't have to leave all their great recipes behind because the times have changed. I can enjoy my grits and still do right by my body! Now that's a deal I think I can live with. In fact, that's a deal I think I can live *better* with. And I surely do hope this book can do the same for you.

From Mama's Table to Mine

CHAPTER 1

When's Dinner?!
Some Favorite Appetizers

YOU KNOW THAT TIME OF THE DAY in the late afternoon when it's not quite dinnertime but your stomach just won't seem to believe you? I reckon that is just about the most dangerous time for trying to eat right. On the other hand, it's also a chance to eat some of the most delicious food of the day. Because that's the hour I start setting out appetizers. These first bites are some of my favorite foods, and I don't like to deprive myself of a good eating opportunity. So I've devised ways to be smart about what I choose at this time of the day.

I like to look at my appetizers as the first part of my evening meal. I mean, what is an appetizer besides the lead-in to the main course? It should work with my main meal, not against it. My first course does the job of getting my appetite in the right frame of mind for what's coming next. If I know what my main meal is going to be, I know what best to pair it up with on the appetizer end.

What I try to do is match a lighter-style appetizer with a heavier meal, and vice versa. If my main meal is going to be something like Grilled Filet Mignon with Vidalia Onions (page 64), I may decide on something like Pickled Shrimp (page 6) to start with. With an ice-cold beer in hand, these babies are a nice bright snack to keep me satisfied as the grill heats up. If I'm planning on something a little lighter for dinner, like Glazed Scallops with Pineapple Salsa (page 80), I may just go with something a little heavier to get me going, like Fiery Queso Fundido (page 12) or Sweet and Savory Meatballs (page 17).

And when I've got friends over for dinner, there's nothing more hospitable than starting the meal out with some really special appetizers. Setting out some beautiful, bite-size Mini Savannah Crab Cakes (page 14) or Spinach-and-Cheese–Stuffed Mushrooms (page 16) tells them my Mama raised me right.

As an added bonus, these recipes are fast and easy to pull together. In fact, most can be finished off before your guests even knock at the door, making for more relaxed entertaining. With these appetizers in your lineup, you'll find yourself free to leave the kitchen, mingle with your guests, and get in a few more bites of each tasty morsel of food you put out.

Bobby's Pimiento Cheese

Well, I guess we Deens are pretty well known for our pimiento cheese at this point. We just love it. That's why a book of healthy comfort food recipes with my name on it absolutely had to include a lighter version of this Southern classic. No matter what you do with it—spread it between two pieces of bread, slather it on top of a burger, or just serve it as is with some vegetable sticks for dipping—this recipe is one you're going to want in your collection. **Makes about 2 cups / Serves 8 to 10**

In the bowl of an electric mixer fitted with the paddle attachment, or using a handheld mixer, beat the cream cheese until fluffy. Beat in the Cheddar, mayonnaise, pimientos, Worcestershire sauce, onion powder, and pepper until well blended. Serve with celery sticks or any vegetable you like.

2 ounces low-fat cream cheese (Neufchâtel), softened

2 cups grated low-fat Cheddar cheese

1/3 cup light mayonnaise

2 tablespoons chopped pimientos, mashed with a fork

1/2 teaspoon Worcestershire sauce

Pinch of onion powder

Freshly ground black pepper to taste

Celery sticks, for serving

My Motivation

Pimiento cheese is my pick-me-up food. When I'm lacking the motivation to get myself moving to do some exercise, I promise myself a pimiento cheese sandwich as a reward for a hard workout. While it may sound funny, just having a goal in front of me makes me work that much harder. Find your own pick-me-up food and use it the next time you need a little extra motivation in keeping healthy.

BREAKIN' IT DOWN

	Before	After
Fat	26g	3g
Calories	316	78

7g protein | 2g carbohydrate
0g fiber | 232mg sodium

Based on 9 servings, does not include celery sticks for serving

Pickled Shrimp

This is a true Low-Country classic, made even quicker and easier by using precooked shrimp. While my Mama keeps her pickled shrimp in pretty little mason jars, I make my mix up and marinate everything the modern way, in a resealable plastic bag. Be sure to pickle your shrimp for at least twenty-four hours to give the flavors time to soak in. The pickled shrimp will last about a week in your fridge, so you can be sure that you'll never get caught out with nothing to serve when friends drop in for a visit.
Serves 6

1 pound cooked, peeled and deveined medium shrimp, with tails

½ small red onion, cut in half lengthwise, then cut crosswise into thin slices

½ medium yellow bell pepper, cut in half lengthwise, then cut crosswise into thin slices

¾ cup fresh lime juice

½ cup white wine vinegar

1 jalapeño, seeded, if desired, and sliced into thin rings

1 tablespoon black peppercorns

½ teaspoon dried oregano

½ teaspoon salt

¼ teaspoon dried minced garlic

Put the shrimp, red onions, bell peppers, lime juice, vinegar, jalapeños, peppercorns, oregano, salt, and garlic into a gallon-size resealable plastic bag along with ¾ cup water. Seal the bag and turn it over a few times to mix the flavors together. Have a quick taste of the marinade and add a pinch or two more salt, if you like. Seal it up again, place the bag in a medium bowl, and refrigerate overnight, turning occasionally. To serve the shrimp, just empty the entire contents of the bag into a big serving bowl and let your guests dig in.

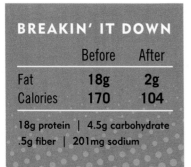

BREAKIN' IT DOWN

	Before	After
Fat	18g	2g
Calories	170	104

18g protein | 4.5g carbohydrate
.5g fiber | 201mg sodium

Tails It Is

There are two reasons I keep the tails on my pickled shrimp. First off, I think it just looks a whole lot better. But more important, with the tails left on, you've got something to grab on to and no need for fiddly toothpicks. And, trust me, when this shrimp is brought out, there will be a whole lot of grabbing going on.

It's a Party Guacamole

Game day can be the downfall of anyone's healthy diet. The temptations are just too great, y'all! But with this guac, I can enjoy the game with my buddies and still feel good about what I've eaten. I make sure to serve this with some healthy dipping options like veggie sticks or baked tortilla chips so that I don't blow it all on the fried chips. **Makes 1½ cups / Serves 6**

2 ripe avocados, pitted, peeled, and finely chopped

¾ cup fat-free sour cream (or use low-fat; optional)

½ teaspoon lime juice

½ teaspoon salt

¼ teaspoon ground cumin

Pinch of cayenne pepper

⅓ cup finely chopped tomatoes

3 tablespoons thinly sliced scallions (white and light green parts only)

¼ cup shredded low-fat Mexican cheese blend

Veggie sticks or baked tortilla chips, for dipping

Using the back of a fork, mash the avocados in a medium bowl. Stir in the sour cream, lime juice, salt, cumin, and cayenne. Scoop the mixture into a serving bowl and sprinkle with the tomatoes, scallions, and Mexican cheese blend. Serve with veggie sticks or baked tortilla chips.

BREAKIN' IT DOWN

	Before	After
Fat	22g	8g
Calories	262	112

3g protein | 10g carbohydrate
13g fiber | 280mg sodium

Shore Is Good Seafood Dip

If you're from Savannah, chances are you've enjoyed a version of this dip at most gatherings you've been to. And if you've ever been to our restaurant, The Lady & Sons, I sure hope you had the opportunity to sample it there. This here is a version you can feel good about treating yourself to any old day of the week. **Makes 6 cups / Serves 12 to 16**

1. Preheat the oven to 325°F. Lightly spray a 2-quart casserole with cooking spray.

2. In a large nonstick skillet coated with cooking spray, cook the celery, bell pepper, and onions over medium heat until the bell peppers and onions begin to soften, 3 to 5 minutes.

3. In a medium bowl, mix together the crabmeat, shrimp, Parmesan, yogurt, mayonnaise, evaporated milk, lemon juice, Worcestershire sauce, paprika, and pepper to taste. Stir in the cooked vegetables from the skillet. Scrape into the prepared casserole and bake for 30 minutes, or until warmed through.

2 celery stalks, finely chopped

1 medium yellow bell pepper, finely chopped

1 medium onion, finely chopped

8 ounces lump crabmeat, picked over to remove bits of shell

8 ounces cooked, peeled, and deveined shrimp, coarsely chopped

1 cup grated Parmesan cheese

½ cup fat-free Greek yogurt (or use low-fat; optional)

½ cup light mayonnaise

2 tablespoons 2% evaporated milk

1 tablespoon fresh lemon juice

1 tablespoon Worcestershire sauce

½ teaspoon paprika

White pepper to taste

Take Your Lumps

I like to splurge and use lump crabmeat in this dip because it contains the sweetest, most tender meat of the crab. By using this high-quality meat, you don't need to dress it up too much with added fat and sugar. It's so tasty on its own, you'll want its great flavor to shine through.

BREAKIN' IT DOWN

	Before	After
Fat	20g	4g
Calories	205	94

10g protein | 4g carbohydrate
0g fiber | 315mg sodium

Gather Round Artichoke and Spinach Dip

If you like your dips decadently cheesy and lusciously creamy, then this is the dip for you. I like to make my own pita crackers to serve alongside. Cut up healthy whole-grain pitas into triangles, give them a spray with some cooking spray, and sprinkle them with sea salt. Then pop them into a 400°F oven for 5 to 7 minutes to crisp up. They're supereasy and a great alternative to higher-calorie options. **Makes 4 cups / Serves 12**

2 cans (14 ounces each) artichoke hearts, drained and chopped

1 package (10 ounces) frozen spinach, thawed, drained, and squeezed dry

1 cup grated Parmesan cheese

1 cup fat-free Greek yogurt (or use low-fat; optional)

½ cup light mayonnaise

1 garlic clove, finely chopped

Freshly ground black pepper to taste

Veggie sticks or healthy crackers, for dipping

1. Preheat the oven to 375°F. Lightly spray a 1½-quart casserole with cooking spray.

2. In a medium bowl, combine the artichokes, spinach, ¾ cup of the Parmesan, the yogurt, mayonnaise, garlic, and pepper to taste. Spoon the mixture into the prepared casserole and sprinkle with the remaining ¼ cup Parmesan. Bake until golden and bubbly, 30 to 40 minutes. Serve with veggie sticks or healthy crackers for dipping.

BREAKIN' IT DOWN

	Before	After
Fat	31g	4g
Calories	650	86

6g protein | 7g carbohydrate
1g fiber | 414mg sodium

Does not include veggie sticks or healthy crackers for dipping

Flavors That Pop

My Mama and my Aunt Peggy used to add a healthy dose of hot sauce to their artichoke dips. If you go in for a little spice, go ahead and shake some in the mix here. But be careful—besides a kick, hot sauce is a hidden source of sodium.

Fiery Queso Fundido

Made with just four simple ingredients, this warm dip is brimming with true Mexican flavor. I like to use a hot, hot salsa in my fundido, but feel free to go milder if that's how you like it. Just be sure to use the fresh salsa you find in the refrigerator case at your supermarket, (not the jarred kind in the chip aisle). You can taste a world of difference between the two. **Makes 4 cups / Serves 10**

2 cups fresh salsa (from the refrigerator case)

1 package (8 ounces) fat-free cream cheese (or use low-fat; optional), softened

1 package (8 ounces) shredded low-fat Mexican cheese blend

1 can (4 ounces) sliced jalapeños

1. Preheat the oven to 400°F and position a rack in the upper third of the oven.

2. In a medium bowl, combine the salsa, cream cheese, and Mexican cheese. Blend and mix well. Scrape into a shallow 1½-quart baking dish and top with the jalapeños. Bake for 30 minutes, or until golden and bubbly.

BREAKIN' IT DOWN

	Before	After
Fat	19g	2g
Calories	241	63

6g protein | 4g carbohydrate
1g fiber | 560mg sodium

Fat-Free Flavor

Sprinkle on some fresh cilantro when you put this dip out. The cilantro adds another level of great Southwest flavor and it looks nice, too. I tend to sprinkle fresh herbs on most dishes just before I dig in. It's a great way to up the flavor of the dish without adding calories.

Hush Puppies

Hush puppies, sweet and spicy dip, and a cold beer. Now that is a recipe for a good night. And this recipe will help you keep your calorie count down, leaving room for that beer. Or maybe even two. **Makes about 2 dozen / Serves 8**

1. Preheat the oven to 450°F. Lightly spray a rimmed baking sheet with cooking spray.

2. In a medium bowl, combine the cornmeal, flour, baking powder, salt, and cayenne.

In a separate bowl, mix together the milk, eggs, oil, and chives. Fold the milk mixture into the cornmeal mixture until the dry ingredients are just moistened.

3. Spoon tablespoon-size dollops of the batter onto the prepared baking sheet, about 1 inch apart. Bake for 10 minutes, or until the hush puppies are firm to the touch and golden brown around the edges.

⅔ cup fine cornmeal

⅓ cup all-purpose flour

1 teaspoon baking powder

¾ teaspoon salt

⅛ teaspoon cayenne pepper

⅓ cup 1% milk

2 large eggs, lightly beaten

1 tablespoon canola oil

⅓ cup finely chopped fresh chives

Take a Dip

I usually serve my hush puppies with a sweet and spicy dipping sauce. I stay away from the overly sweetened dips you may find on the supermarket shelves and make my own. I mix together some freshly squeezed orange juice with just the tiniest amount of marmalade to thicken it up, along with a dash of low-sodium soy sauce and some freshly sliced jalapeño for a good kick.

BREAKIN' IT DOWN

	Before	After
Fat	13g	3g
Calories	277	93

3g protein | 12g carbohydrate
1g fiber | 242 mg sodium

Mini Savannah Crab Cakes

In Savannah, I reckon there are about as many opinions on crab cakes as there are people. A few things we all agree on, though, are that they should be loaded with crabmeat, light on the bread crumbs, and spiced with Old Bay. In short, they should taste like they just jumped out of the sea. Hit them with a squeeze of lemon just before serving and you've got yourself a surefire winner. **Makes 8 to 10 / Serves 4**

8 ounces fresh or canned lump crabmeat, drained if canned

6 tablespoons dried bread crumbs

2 tablespoons finely chopped scallions (white and light green parts only)

2 tablespoons light mayonnaise

1 jalapeño, seeded and finely chopped

1 large egg white, lightly beaten

1 teaspoon Old Bay seasoning

1 teaspoon Dijon mustard

1 lemon, cut into wedges, for serving

1. In a large bowl, stir together the crabmeat, 3 tablespoons of the bread crumbs, the scallions, mayonnaise, jalapeños, egg white, Old Bay, and mustard.

2. Form the mixture into 1½-inch patties. Place the remaining 3 tablespoons bread crumbs in a bowl. Dip each crab cake in the bread crumbs to lightly coat. Spray a skillet generously with cooking spray and place over medium-high heat. Cook the crab cakes in batches, until golden, 2 to 3 minutes per side. To prevent sticking, spray the skillet with more cooking spray between batches.

BREAKIN' IT DOWN

	Before	After
Fat	6g	1g
Calories	136	30

13g protein | 10g carbohydrate
1g fiber | 617mg sodium

Trim Tartar

If you'd like to serve these crab cakes with a dipping sauce, you can whip up a quick, lighter-style tartar sauce. Just substitute low-fat yogurt for the mayonnaise. You can mix in a tablespoon or two of low-fat mayonnaise to give it some body. To skip the extra sugar, use chopped-up pickles instead of pickle relish. Then mix in some fresh herbs like parsley or tarragon to give it a fresh flavor.

Spinach-and-Cheese–Stuffed Mushrooms

This is one of my favorite appetizers that my Mama makes. She packs hers with feta and spinach because she knows I just can't get enough of that combo. So all I needed to do here was cut the fat a bit by swapping in low-fat sour cream for the cream cheese. Oh, and I upped the feta because, in my book, you can't ever have too much cheese. **Makes about 3 dozen / Serves 12**

1 package (10 ounces) frozen chopped spinach, thawed, drained, and squeezed dry

1½ cups crumbled feta cheese

½ cup finely chopped scallions (white and light green parts only)

¼ cup low-fat sour cream

½ teaspoon The Lady's House Seasoning (recipe below)

1½ pounds white mushrooms (about 36), stems removed

¼ cup grated Parmesan cheese

1. Preheat the oven to 375°F and position a rack in the upper third of the oven.

2. In a medium bowl, combine the spinach, feta, scallions, sour cream, and House Seasoning and stir well. Fill the mushroom caps with the mixture and top with the Parmesan. Place the mushrooms on a rimmed baking sheet and bake for 15 to 20 minutes, until the topping is golden.

A Gentle Touch

You need a soft touch in removing the stems from white mushrooms so you don't tear into your mushroom caps. I suggest using a gentle back-and-forth motion on the stem until it literally pops out. You want those mushroom caps intact so they provide a clean little bowl for your filling. To clean mushrooms, never soak them in water. They are very porous, so you don't want them filling up with water. If they aren't too dirty, just give them a gentle wipe with a dry paper towel. For dirtier mushrooms, go ahead and use a damp paper towel.

The Lady's House Seasoning

While you can certainly buy a bottle of our Paula Deen House Seasoning, it's also really easy to make up yourself. Here's the recipe, y'all. I highly recommend you add it to your spice collection.

1 cup salt
¼ cup freshly ground black pepper
¼ cup garlic powder

Combine all the ingredients in a small bowl. Store in an airtight container for up to 6 months. Makes 1½ cups.

BREAKIN' IT DOWN

	Before	After
Fat	14g	5g
Calories	138	85

6g protein | 4g carbohydrate
1g fiber | 157mg sodium

Sweet and Savory Meatballs

This hearty appetizer is a real crowd-pleaser. When I've got a few friends over for a sit-down dinner, I like to serve these superflavorful meatballs in small, deep bowls, with lots of sauce drizzled over and plenty of fresh parsley sprinkled on top. If I'm having a bigger crowd over for lots of finger food, I serve these up on a big platter with toothpicks for people to spear them with. **Makes 40 / Serves 8**

1. In a medium bowl, combine the beef, ricotta, raisins, salt, and pepper and mix gently. Roll into forty 1-inch meatballs.

2. Spray a large nonstick skillet with cooking spray and place over medium heat. Add the meatballs in batches and brown on all sides, 7 to 8 minutes total. Set the meatballs aside on a plate.

3. Add the onions to the skillet and cook, stirring, until browned, 2 to 3 minutes. Add the tomato sauce and vinegar and bring to a gentle boil. Return the meatballs to the pan and cook, stirring carefully to coat with sauce, for 5 minutes, until cooked through. Serve the meatballs in small bowls topped with a generous amount of the sauce and a sprinkling of the parsley.

1 pound 95% lean ground beef

½ cup fat-free ricotta cheese (or use low-fat; optional)

½ cup raisins, coarsely chopped

¾ teaspoon salt

¼ teaspoon freshly ground black pepper

½ cup finely chopped onion

1 can (15 ounces) low-sodium tomato sauce

1 tablespoon balsamic vinegar

¼ cup coarsely chopped fresh parsley, for serving

Raisin Right

I think I'm gonna surprise y'all with this little fact. Raisins are something of a nutritional powerhouse. They are packed with vitamins and minerals, are high in fiber, low in sodium, and are a natural source of sugar. I love them in these meatballs. They add just the right amount of sweetness to the dish.

BREAKIN' IT DOWN

	Before	After
Fat	10g	2g
Calories	193	121

12g protein | 12g carbohydrate
1g fiber | 273mg sodium

Easy Ginger-Glazed Spareribs

These Asian-style sweet and tangy ribs will have your guests licking their fingers with gusto. I can't think of another appetizer that is so easy to prepare yet tastes so lip-smacking good. No matter what style of ribs you prepare, they always seem to bring the party with them. **Serves 12 (about 3 riblets per person)**

3 pounds Chinese-style pork spareribs, trimmed of excess fat

1½ teaspoons salt

¾ teaspoon freshly ground black pepper

3 tablespoons molasses

1 tablespoon ketchup

2 teaspoons low-sodium soy sauce

2 teaspoons peeled and finely chopped fresh ginger

2 teaspoons sherry vinegar

1 garlic clove, finely chopped

1. Using a sharp knife, cut and pull the white membrane from the bony side of the rack of ribs. Season the ribs all over with the salt and pepper. Cover loosely with plastic wrap and refrigerate for 3 hours.

2. In a small bowl, make the glaze by stirring together the molasses, ketchup, soy sauce, ginger, vinegar, and garlic until combined. Cover and refrigerate until ready to use.

3. Preheat the oven to 325°F.

4. Place the ribs, bony side down, on a foil-lined rimmed baking sheet. Cover tightly with foil. Bake for 1½ hours. Uncover and brush the ribs lightly with half of the prepared glaze. Bake, uncovered, 15 minutes. Baste with the remaining glaze and continue to bake until the rib meat is very tender and the glaze is sticky, about 15 minutes more. Test for doneness by poking a fork between the bones. If the fork inserts easily, the ribs are done. Let them stand for 10 minutes before cutting them into individual ribs.

BREAKIN' IT DOWN

	Before	After
Fat	43g	28g
Calories	547	320

19g protein | 4g carbohydrate
0g fiber | 415mg sodium

CHAPTER 2

Soup's On!

SO COMFORTING, TASTY, AND WARM—soup is the ultimate one-pot meal, packed with protein and vitamins, and, most important, satisfying flavor. My favorite meal after a good workout is piping-hot soup. Just one hearty bowl has the power to replace all the nutrients I've worked off at the gym, without making me feel stuffed.

I make sure I always have homemade soup in the fridge or freezer. That way I'm not tempted to pick up a canned soup at the market. Canned soups tend to contain lots of sodium, something I'm really trying to cut down on in my diet. If I've made the soup, I know exactly what's gone into it. The fact is, soups are so easy to make and they go a good long way. I like to call them my fridge and pantry cleaners. Whatever I've got on hand goes right into the pot. And when I make soup, I make loads of it. Tell me, who doesn't like soup even better when it's served the next day, having given the flavors time to build? What's not to love about a meal that cooks up all in one pot? Less washing up means more quality time spent on the things I love to do.

Beyond what's in the fridge and pantry, soup should be about what's fresh and looks good at the market. Come the months of November and December when squash is so plentiful and inexpensive it's practically being given away, I like to enjoy Secret Ingredient Butternut Squash Soup (page 25). Sweet and creamy, it's like a warm blanket on a cold winter day. And my secret ingredient gives this soup an extra kick of protein. But you'll just have to wait until you turn to that recipe to find out what that is.

A sentimental favorite soup of mine is Jack's Corn Chowder (page 28). I make a lighter version of the soup my Mama created for my brother Jamie's son Jack. But don't be fooled. It may be named for my little nephew because it's his favorite, but this soup is definitely not child's play. It will satisfy even the most discerning adult appetite. It was a cinch to lighten up because it turned out I didn't need the cream or flour to thicken it up. Potatoes make a great no-fat soup thickener. As a result, this soup is packed with flavor but has way fewer calories and cholesterol.

From the most humble foods come the most delicious soups. Inexpensive cuts of meat that positively fall apart, earthy root vegetables, and aromatic spices—these are the ingredients that make soups that are bursting with flavor. When you've got homemade soup in the house, why, you've got yourself a warm hug just waiting for you every time you open the fridge.

Tomato Soup with Cheddar Croutons

This recipe is a play on the classic duo of tomato soup with a grilled cheese sandwich served alongside. Here the grilled cheese comes in the form of homemade cheesy croutons, only made a whole lot better for you. The tomato soup is thick, creamy, and subtly spiced, just right on a chilly day. **Serves 4**

1. To make the croutons: Preheat the oven to 425°F.

2. Pour the baking mix into a medium bowl and use your hands to incorporate the butter substitute until the mixture has the consistency of sand. Add the milk and ¼ cup of the Cheddar. Stir together to incorporate, then knead with the palm of your hand 4 to 5 times to form a stiff dough. Turn the dough out onto a lightly floured surface and roll and pat into a 4 by 6-inch rectangle. Cut into six 2-inch squares, place on an ungreased rimmed baking sheet, and top with the remaining ¼ cup cheese.

3. Bake for 10 minutes, or until lightly golden brown. Let cool on a wire rack, then cut each piece into 4 squares to give you 24 croutons.

4. To make the soup: Spray a nonstick soup pot with cooking spray and place over medium heat. Add the onions and cook until translucent, 3 to 5 minutes. Add the tomatoes, chicken broth, evaporated milk, basil, marjoram, and pepper to taste and bring to a boil over medium-high heat. Reduce the heat to medium-low and let simmer for 10 minutes. Puree the soup using a blender, food processor, or immersion blender. Serve topped with the croutons.

Croutons

1 cup whole-wheat baking mix (such as Bisquick)

1 tablespoon low-calorie butter substitute spread

¼ cup 1% milk

½ cup grated low-fat Cheddar cheese

Soup

1 cup finely chopped onions

1 can (14½ ounces) low-sodium diced tomatoes

1½ cups low-sodium chicken broth

½ cup fat-free evaporated milk (or use low-fat; optional)

¼ teaspoon dried basil

¼ teaspoon dried marjoram

Freshly ground black pepper to taste

Immerse Yourself

If you haven't already got an immersion blender, I highly recommend picking yourself up one. It is inexpensive and super-handy for pureeing soups, mixing up batters, and whipping up quick smoothies (a great pre-workout energy booster). And since it blends right there in the pot or bowl your ingredients are sitting in, it means less mess.

BREAKIN' IT DOWN

	Before	After
Fat	23g	5g
Calories	470	224

12g protein | 35g carbohydrate
4g fiber | 504mg sodium

The Son's Chicken Noodle Soup

I swear that my Mama's chicken noodle soup could knock a cold out of you in two spoonfuls. Her homemade chicken broth is sensational, but it's a little time consuming for midweek. When I feel a cold coming on, I whip up this quick version of Mama's soup, using a good-quality low-sodium chicken broth from the market. I've added fresh oregano and lemon zest to my soup to give it a fresh, bright flavor.
Makes 12 cups / Serves 10

2 tablespoons olive oil

3 medium carrots, cut into ¼-inch slices (about 2 cups)

2 large celery stalks, cut into ¼-inch slices (about 2 cups)

1 medium onion, coarsely chopped

1 garlic clove, finely chopped

8 cups low-sodium chicken broth

1 tablespoon coarsely chopped fresh oregano or dill (optional)

2 bay leaves

Freshly ground black pepper to taste

1 pound boneless, skinless chicken breasts, cut into ½-inch pieces

1 teaspoon grated lemon zest

4 ounces medium egg noodles

¼ cup grated Parmesan cheese

¼ cup coarsely chopped fresh parsley

1. In a large soup pot, heat the oil over medium-high heat. Add the carrots, celery, and onions and cook, stirring occasionally, until the onion is softened, 5 to 7 minutes. Add the garlic and cook for 30 seconds. Add the chicken broth, oregano, bay leaves, and pepper. Bring to a gentle boil and cook until the carrots are easily pierced with a fork, 2 to 3 minutes. Add the chicken and lemon zest and return to a boil. Add the noodles and cook until the noodles are tender, about 7 minutes.

2. Stir in the Parmesan and parsley, and ladle into bowls.

BREAKIN' IT DOWN

	Before	After
Fat	22g	6g
Calories	421	162

16g protein | 14g carbohydrate
1g fiber | 255mg sodium

Quick Freeze

I make fast work of cutting up the chicken for this soup by placing it in the freezer for about 20 minutes before I take a knife to it. That way it doesn't slip around on the cutting board and I can make nice clean cuts.

Secret Ingredient Butternut Squash Soup

This sweet, savory, velvety soup is special enough to serve right alongside a holiday dinner. But it's healthy enough to serve every day. By adding tofu, I've managed to up the ante on the protein count. And that's exactly what I need after an intense workout. But, if it's all the same to you, I'm going to keep the tofu thing from the guys at the gym. **Makes 11 cups / Serves 6 to 8**

1. In a medium pot, heat the oil and butter over medium heat. Add the onions and cook until softened, about 5 minutes. Add the squash, apples, chicken broth, and thyme. Then add the tofu, breaking it into pieces with a wooden spoon. Bring to a boil, then lower the heat and let the soup simmer, partially covered, until the squash is very soft, about 20 minutes.

2. Puree the soup using a blender, food processor, or immersion blender. If necessary, return the soup to the pot to warm up and season to taste with pepper. Serve with a healthy dollop of yogurt and sprinkle on a little cinnamon.

1 tablespoon olive oil

1 tablespoon unsalted butter

1 medium onion, coarsely chopped

1 medium butternut squash, peeled, seeded, and cut into 1-inch chunks (3 cups)

1 medium apple, peeled, cored, and coarsely chopped

5 cups low-sodium chicken broth

¼ teaspoon dried thyme

1 container (14 ounces) soft tofu, drained

Freshly ground black pepper

2% Greek yogurt, for serving

Ground cinnamon, for serving

Refuel the Body

You know those post-workout energy drinks that are out there on the market shelves? They basically contain a ton of protein and carbohydrates that are great to get back into your body immediately after a workout. Post-workout is the best time to load up on protein and carbs because your body sends them to your muscles instead of storing it in your fat reserves. Well, guess what? This soup is another version of an energy drink. Spoon this up after your workout and you'll get all the same benefits along with your lunch.

BREAKIN' IT DOWN

	Before	After
Fat	14g	7g
Calories	266	141

8g protein | 14g carbohydrate 2g fiber | 60mg sodium

Nutritional count based on 7 servings; does not include Greek yogurt for serving

Oyster Stew

I know oysters are the food of love, so you'd think this would be the official soup of Valentine's Day. But in my house when I was growing up, this is the soup we'd enjoy on Thanksgiving. It's an old New Orleans tradition to have this soup on Thanksgiving Day, and the soup is a silky, salty, briny knockout. Here's something you can really be thankful for: My oyster stew has only 233 calories and 8 grams of fat. Amen to that. **Makes 6 cups / Serves 4**

1 tablespoon unsalted butter

¼ cup coarsely chopped scallions (white and light green parts only)

12 ounces shucked raw oysters, with their liquor (juices)

3 cups fat-free half-and-half (or use low-fat; optional)

⅛ teaspoon salt

Pinch of cayenne pepper

Freshly ground black pepper to taste

1 cup oyster crackers

1. In a medium pot, melt the butter over medium heat. Add the scallions and cook until softened. Stir in the oysters with their liquor, the half-and-half, salt, cayenne, and black pepper. Simmer over low heat until the edges of the oysters begin to curl and the mixture is hot, but not boiling, about 3 minutes.

2. Ladle the soup into four bowls and spoon ¼ cup of the crackers on top of each serving.

BREAKIN' IT DOWN

	Before	After
Fat	19g	8g
Calories	316	233

11g protein | 28g carbohydrate
.5g fiber | 544mg sodium

Runnin' on Empty

Want to stock your pantry with the right foods? Take my advice. Never go to the supermarket on an empty stomach. Food shopping when you're hungry leads to all sorts of impulse buys. And I can guarantee they won't be healthy. So, treat yourself to a satisfying meal first. Then work it off by pushing that shopping cart around.

Broccoli Cheese Soup

Broccoli and Cheddar cheese is one of those pairings that was made in heaven. They taste so darn good together. When I was young, pairing them up was the only way my Mama got me to eat my broccoli. These days I enjoy the combo in a hearty, warming soup that's positively brimming over with melted, gooey cheese. **Makes 8 cups / Serves 4**

1. In a large pot, heat the oil over medium heat. Add the onions and cook, stirring, until soft, about 5 minutes. Stir in the flour, garlic powder, and salt and cook for 2 minutes.

2. Slowly whisk in the chicken broth and simmer the liquid until it thickens slightly. Add the broccoli and cook until tender, 7 to 10 minutes.

3. Remove the soup from the heat and puree using a blender, food processor, or immersion blender. If necessary, return the soup to the pot and heat over medium heat. Whisk in the milk, 1 cup of the Cheddar, and the pepper. Ladle the soup into serving bowls and sprinkle each with 1 tablespoon of the remaining cheese.

2 teaspoons olive oil

1 medium onion, finely chopped

3 tablespoons all-purpose flour

½ teaspoon garlic powder

¼ teaspoon salt

3 cups low-sodium chicken broth

6 cups broccoli florets

1 cup 2% milk

1¼ cups grated low-fat sharp Cheddar cheese

Freshly ground black pepper to taste

Flour Power

The flour in this recipe helps to thicken up the soup nicely. Just make sure you cook the flour off for a couple minutes before you add the broth. By cooking your flour off, your soup won't end up tasting of raw flour.

BREAKIN' IT DOWN

	Before	After
Fat	19g	8g
Calories	309	245

20g protein | 28g carbohydrate
7g fiber | 529mg sodium

Jack's Corn Chowder

When my nephew Jack was a toddler, we sure had our challenges getting him to eat the right foods. My Mama was constantly whipping up new recipes to get him to eat more vegetables. This one sure did the trick. Jack fell head over heels for her corn chowder, and so it was only right to name it after him. My version of Jack's chowder is fantastically thick and creamy. And it doesn't contain a lick of cream! I can get away with using only milk because the pureed potatoes provide a great no-fat thickener. **Makes 6 cups / Serves 6**

1 tablespoon low-calorie butter substitute spread

½ cup finely chopped onions

½ cup finely chopped carrots

¼ cup finely chopped celery

1 garlic clove, finely chopped

3 cups fresh or frozen corn kernels

2 cups low-sodium chicken broth

1 small potato, peeled and cut into chunks

1½ cups whole milk

Pinch of nutmeg, preferably freshly grated

White pepper to taste

1. In a medium pot, melt the butter substitute over medium heat. Add the onions, carrots, and celery and cook, stirring frequently, until the onions are softened, 3 to 5 minutes. Add the garlic and cook for 30 seconds. Add the corn and chicken broth and bring to a boil over medium-high heat. Lower the heat and simmer for 10 minutes.

2. Remove 1 cup of the soup and puree in a blender or food processor; return the pureed soup to the pot.

3. Meanwhile, in a small saucepan, cover the potatoes with cold salted water. Bring to a boil over medium-high heat and cook until the potatoes are easily pierced with a fork, about 20 minutes. Drain and place in a blender or food processor. Add the milk and puree until smooth.

4. Add the potato mixture to the soup and season with nutmeg and pepper.

BREAKIN' IT DOWN

	Before	After
Fat	**13g**	**2g**
Calories	**255**	**131**

6g protein | 25g carbohydrate
3g fiber | 178mg sodium

For the Grown-ups

If I'm not making this soup for my nephews, I like to throw a jalapeño in there for an extra kick. Jalapeño goes great with potato and really cuts through the creamy texture to add another level of flavor.

French Onion Soup

This onion soup may have come to us from the French, but my version puts a little Georgia spin on it. The Vidalia onions make this soup sweet and mellow and oh so delicious. **Makes 6 cups / Serves 4**

2 large Vidalia or other sweet onions

2 teaspoons unsalted butter

1 teaspoon sugar

½ teaspoon salt

3 cups low-sodium beef broth

¼ cup dry red wine

1 teaspoon dried thyme

4 thin slices whole-wheat baguette, toasted

4 ounces grated low-fat Swiss cheese (1 cup)

Freshly ground black pepper to taste

1. Thinly slice one of the onions; finely chop the second. In a medium pot, melt the butter over medium heat. Add the sliced onions, sugar, and ¼ teaspoon of the salt. Cover and cook until almost soft, about 10 minutes. Add the chopped onions, increase the heat to medium-high, cover, and cook until the onions are well caramelized, 10 to 15 minutes more.

2. Stir the beef broth, red wine, thyme, and the remaining ¼ teaspoon salt into the pot. Simmer gently for 10 minutes.

3. Preheat the broiler.

4. Ladle the soup into four heatproof bowls. Float 1 baguette slice in each bowl and sprinkle the cheese over the top. Cook under the broiler until the cheese is golden and bubbling, about 5 minutes. Season to taste with pepper.

BREAKIN' IT DOWN

	Before	After
Fat	16g	5g
Calories	270	192

14g protein | 10g carbohydrate
1g fiber | 490mg sodium

Add a Side Salad

Turn this soup into a satisfying meal by pairing it up with a green salad. Grab one of those bags of prewashed mixed baby lettuce leaves and shake up a dressing of whole-grain mustard, white wine vinegar, and a little olive oil. Bon appétit!

The Son's Beef Vegetable Soup

Now here's a soup I like to cook up in a big batch, giving me enough to save leftovers in the freezer. Only problem is, I find myself so enjoying this hearty, stick-to-your-ribs soup that I eat my leftovers before they even make it to the freezer. The meat is so fall-apart tender it will melt in your mouth. And a bowl of this tasty soup is jam-packed with veggies, giving you plenty to feel good about. **Makes 18 cups / Serves 12**

1. In a large soup pot, heat the oil over medium-high heat. Season the beef with the salt and pepper to taste. Working in batches, brown the beef all over. Set aside the browned meat on a plate.

2. Add the onions and celery to the pot and cook until the vegetables are softened, about 5 minutes. Stir in the garlic powder, tomatoes, beef broth, 2 cups water, and the bay leaves. Return the beef and its juices to the pot and simmer, uncovered, until very tender, 1½ to 2 hours. Add the potatoes for the last 30 minutes of this cooking time.

3. When the meat is tender, stir in the frozen vegetables, butter beans, and peas and simmer for 10 minutes. Stir in the Worcestershire sauce just before serving.

1 tablespoon olive oil

2 pounds boneless chuck, cut into 1½-inch pieces

1 teaspoon salt

Freshly ground black pepper to taste

1 cup finely chopped onions

1 cup finely chopped celery

1 teaspoon garlic powder

2 cans (14½ ounces each) low-sodium diced tomatoes with Italian seasonings

2 quarts low-sodium beef broth

2 bay leaves

1½ cups peeled and finely chopped potatoes

3 cups frozen mixed vegetables

1½ cups frozen butter beans

1½ cups canned or frozen black-eyed peas, rinsed and drained if canned

1 tablespoon Worcestershire sauce

Tricks of the Trade

Here's a little trick my Mama taught me. To remove excess beef fat that floats to the top of the soup, swirl a large iceberg lettuce leaf around the surface of the soup—the leaf will pick up a lot of the fat.

BREAKIN' IT DOWN

	Before	After
Fat	22g	11g
Calories	581	322

23g protein | 24g carbohydrate
6g fiber | 546mg sodium

Black Bean Soup with Avocado

This hearty soup tastes like a slice of the tropics. I like to serve it with heaps of limes to keep it really bright. If I'm making a meal out of this soup, I may stir in some corn to get even more fresh vegetable flavor. Then I place a helping of brown rice in a bowl and ladle the soup right over it. **Makes 6 cups / Serves 4**

1 tablespoon olive oil

1 small onion, finely chopped

2 garlic cloves, finely chopped

1 teaspoon chili powder

2 teaspoons ground cumin

2 cans (15 ounces each) black beans, rinsed and drained

1 can (14½ ounces) low-sodium diced tomatoes

½ teaspoon salt

¼ cup fat-free Greek yogurt (or use low-fat; optional), for serving

1 medium avocado, pitted, peeled, and finely chopped, for serving

Lime wedges, for serving

1. In a large pot, heat the oil over medium-high heat. Add the onions and cook until softened, about 5 minutes. Stir in the garlic, chili powder, and cumin and cook for 1 minute. Stir in the beans, tomatoes, 2 cups water, and the salt. Simmer over medium heat for 15 minutes.

2. Ladle the soup into bowls and top with some of the yogurt, avocado, and a squeeze of lime.

BREAKIN' IT DOWN

	Before	After
Fat	15g	10g
Calories	464	233

11g protein | 29g carbohydrate
13g fiber | 383mg sodium

Bean Basics

It's really important that you rinse and drain canned beans before tossing them into the pot. You see, canned beans are packed in brine, which is a salty liquid meant to keep them fresh. By rinsing off the beans first, you'll get rid of this excess salt.

Confederate Bean Soup

This soup is so good, y'all. My Mama's is fantastic too, but she makes hers with canned baked beans, which are loaded with sugar. I replicate that sweet baked bean flavor by adding just a bit of brown sugar. This soup is also packed with sausage, but, remarkably, it's still only 248 calories per serving. **Makes 5 cups / Serves 4**

8 ounces turkey kielbasa

1 medium onion, finely chopped

1 garlic clove, finely chopped

1 can (15½ ounces) small white beans

1 cup low-sodium chicken broth

½ cup canned low-sodium crushed tomatoes

1 teaspoon light brown sugar

¼ teaspoon dry mustard powder

Freshly ground black pepper to taste

½ cup 2% evaporated milk

1. In a medium pot coated with cooking spray, sauté the kielbasa and onions over medium heat until the onions are softened, about 5 minutes. Add the garlic and cook for 30 seconds. Add the beans, chicken broth, tomatoes, brown sugar, mustard powder, and pepper to taste and bring to a boil over medium-high heat. Reduce the heat and simmer, partly covered, for 10 minutes.

2. Remove from the heat, stir in the evaporated milk, and serve.

BREAKIN' IT DOWN

	Before	After
Fat	14g	8g
Calories	459	248

19g protein | 30g carbohydrate
10g fiber | 729mg sodium

Corn Bread Complement

Now, traditionally this soup is served with piping-hot skillet corn bread. If that's what you've got a hankering for, I say go for it. But make sure it's a healthy version, like my Real Southern Corn Bread (page 134). And whatever you do, don't blow your healthy diet by adding a big ol' pat of butter when you serve it up!

CHAPTER 3

Satisfying Salads

A BUSY LIFE DOES NOT HAVE TO MEAN endless dinners of take-out and frozen food. When you're short on time, a great dinner option is a healthy, hearty salad. Now I'm not talking about some iceberg lettuce dressed up with a few tomato and cucumber slices. No, ma'am. I'm talking about a salad that makes you happy. I'm talking about a salad that's loaded with protein, fresh veggies, yummy leftovers from the fridge, and then finished off with a drizzling of a tangy, tasty dressing. I get happy just thinking about it.

My salads serve as satisfying meals containing the meats, cheeses, nuts, and vegetables that I like to eat, along with crisp, bright greens. The sky really is the limit when it comes to salads, and Cornucopia Salad (page 38) is a great example. This pretty layered salad is chock-full of crunchy celery, sweet bananas, salty nuts, plump raisins, and Cheddar cheese, all topped off with crumbled bacon. I've lightened up my Mama's version by using light mayonnaise and fat-free Greek yogurt in my dressing. I tell you, there's everything but the kitchen sink in this salad!

All right, so throwing together some nuts and cheese may sound easy, but what about washing and drying all those salad greens? When I'm really pressed for time, I turn to store-bought prewashed bagged lettuces. They really are one of the great modern conveniences. When I've got a little more time on my hands and I make it to the farmers' market for some fresh-picked leaves, I give all the leaves a good wash as soon as I get home. Then I spin them nice and dry in a salad spinner. The drier the lettuce is after washing, the longer it will last in the fridge. With all my greens washed and dried, when I get a craving for a salad, all I have to do is grab a handful and toss it in a bowl.

When it comes to dressings, I like to mix it up. There are some great bottled dressings out there on the shelves, but most days I like to make my own dressings at home. It's so easy to create outstanding homemade dressings. Take, for instance, the blue cheese dressing in The Lady & Sons Wedge Salad with Blue Cheese and Bacon (page 39). I whisk together Greek yogurt, light mayo, buttermilk, and white wine vinegar with some crumbled blue cheese to create my own restaurant-style dressing. Other times I shake my dressings up in a pretty little crystal cruet a friend of mine gave me, but any empty jelly jar will do the trick.

A satisfying salad is a great way to eat healthy when time is short. Come to think of it, a satisfying salad is a great way to eat healthy just about any old time.

Cornucopia Salad

When I introduced this salad to my friends in New York, there was a fair bit of skepticism around the table. Until they dug in, that is. After that it was all over. Never again will they doubt that an old-fashioned Southern salad can deliver the goods. This salad has everything—sweet raisins and bananas, crisp lettuce and water chestnuts, a tangy creamy dressing, and salty bacon and nuts. This truly is a salad like no other. **Serves 10**

Dressing

2 tablespoons fresh lemon juice

2 tablespoons sugar

1⅓ cups fat-free Greek yogurt (or use low-fat; optional)

¼ cup light mayonnaise

Salad

1 medium head iceberg lettuce, shredded

½ cup coarsely chopped green bell peppers

½ cup coarsely chopped celery

½ cup frozen green peas, thawed

1 can (8 ounces) sliced water chestnuts, drained

2 medium bananas, sliced and tossed with 2 tablespoons fresh lemon juice

½ cup grated low-fat Cheddar cheese

⅓ cup raisins

⅓ cup coarsely chopped nuts (pecans, walnuts, or peanuts)

⅓ cup coarsely chopped scallions (white and light green parts only)

6 bacon slices, cooked crisp and crumbled

1. To make the dressing: In a small bowl, combine the lemon juice and sugar and stir until the sugar has dissolved. Add the yogurt and mayonnaise and stir well. Refrigerate until ready to use.

2. To make the salad: In a 9 by 13-inch baking dish, layer the lettuce, bell peppers, celery, peas, water chestnuts, and bananas. Pour the dressing over the salad and, using the back of a spoon, spread the dressing evenly over the entire salad.

3. In a small bowl, toss together the Cheddar, raisins, and nuts. Scatter the mixture over the top of the dressing. Top with the scallions and bacon and serve.

BREAKIN' IT DOWN

	Before	After
Fat	**36g**	**6g**
Calories	**600**	**156**

8g protein | 17g carbohydrate
3g fiber | 204mg sodium

Nuts about Nuts

To my mind, salty peanuts are the way to go in this salad. The rich, salty flavor of this humble nut balances so nicely with the sweetness of the banana and raisins and the tartness of the lemony dressing. And, by the way, peanuts are loaded with protein. They contain more protein than any other nut out there.

The Lady & Sons Wedge Salad with Blue Cheese and Bacon

I am telling you, this blue cheese dressing is so good, I will not be going back to the full-fat version. It's creamy, luscious, full of flavor, and so good that even my Mama now makes it this way at home. I love to serve this salad paired up with a lean grilled steak. It's so good, y'all! **Serves 4**

1. To make the dressing: In a small bowl, combine the yogurt, blue cheese, mayonnaise, buttermilk, and vinegar and stir well.

2. To make the salad: Place the lettuce wedges on individual plates and top with the dressing and crumbled bacon.

Dressing

½ cup fat-free Greek yogurt (or use low-fat; optional)

½ cup crumbled blue cheese

2 tablespoons light mayonnaise

2 tablespoons 1% buttermilk

1 teaspoon white wine vinegar

Salad

1 small head iceberg lettuce, cut into 4 wedges

4 bacon slices, cooked and crumbled

Dress Down

While salads are a great meal option, it's important to keep an eye on your dressings because they are where you can add a whole heap of extra fat and calories. Use only what you need to lightly coat your salad. And when you're eating out, always ask for the dressing on the side. Restaurants have a tendency to be a little heavy-handed with the dressing.

BREAKIN' IT DOWN

	Before	After
Fat	36g	10g
Calories	428	142

11g protein | 6g carbohydrate
1g fiber | 490mg sodium

Spinach Salad with Warm Bacon Dressing

It doesn't get much better for you than spinach. This leafy green vegetable is a great source of vitamins A, C, E, K, iron, calcium, and folate. And that's just to name a few! I try to have a spinach salad at least once a week. But besides all that, it just plain tastes good. **Serves 4**

12 cups fresh baby spinach

1 cup thinly sliced white mushrooms

6 turkey bacon slices

¼ cup olive oil

½ small red onion, thinly sliced

¼ cup red wine vinegar

1½ teaspoons Dijon mustard

Freshly ground black pepper to taste

1. In a large serving bowl, toss together the spinach and mushrooms, then set aside while you make the dressing.

2. In a large skillet, cook the bacon over medium-low heat until crisp, 5 to 10 minutes. Set the bacon on a paper towel–lined plate to drain.

3. Add the oil and red onions to the skillet and cook for 10 seconds. Whisk in the vinegar and mustard and scrape up any browned bits stuck to the skillet. Crumble in the bacon and cook for 30 seconds.

4. Pour the hot vinaigrette over the spinach and mushrooms. Season with pepper and serve immediately.

BREAKIN' IT DOWN

	Before	After
Fat	25g	18g
Calories	250	198

6g protein | 3g carbohydrate
1g fiber | 174mg sodium

It's in the Bag

Spinach can be a notoriously difficult leaf to clean. That's why I buy my baby spinach in the bag. It comes triple washed, and I've found the quality to be really good. Cutting out the cleaning step helps to ensure that I choose salad over another lunch that may not be as healthy.

New-fashioned Cabbage Slaw

It doesn't get much quicker than this slaw. You can whip it up in about ten minutes' time, let it sit for another ten, then serve it up. But watch out, this slaw tastes so good, you may just devour it in ten minutes flat, too! I love to serve this salad next to just about any smoked or barbecued meat. **Serves 4**

4 cups packaged coleslaw mix

½ cup ¼-inch red bell pepper strips

½ cup ¼-inch yellow bell pepper strips

½ cup very small broccoli florets

¼ cup thinly sliced scallions (white and light green parts only)

¼ cup light mayonnaise

1 teaspoon sugar

½ teaspoon celery seed

1½ teaspoons apple cider vinegar

In a large bowl, combine the coleslaw mix, bell peppers, broccoli, scallions, mayonnaise, sugar, celery seed, and vinegar. Toss well to combine. Let stand for 10 minutes before serving.

BREAKIN' IT DOWN

	Before	After
Fat	10g	3g
Calories	180	71

1g protein | 9g carbohydrate
2g fiber | 100mg sodium

Sandwich Topper

This slaw is great to have in the fridge for topping sandwiches. Southerners like to pile their sandwiches high, and this is one of the best salads for doing just that.

Frozen Waldorf Salad

This is the lightest and most refreshing salad and a true Southern classic on a hot summer day. It feels decadent, just like a frozen treat. But it's not, thanks to my new best friend Greek yogurt, as well as to an old standby, light whipped topping. This salad has even gotten the thumbs-up from my most demanding salad critic, my little nephew Jack. So you know it's gotta be good! **Serves 8 to 10**

1. In the bowl of an electric mixer fitted with the paddle attachment, or using a handheld mixer, mix the yogurt, cream cheese, and pineapple juice at medium speed until smooth. Stir in the crushed pineapple, apple, walnuts, celery, and grapes. Using a rubber spatula, fold the whipped topping into the yogurt mixture. Scrape into an 8-inch square pan, cover with plastic wrap, and freeze for 4 hours or overnight.

2. Remove the salad from the freezer 20 minutes before serving. Cut into squares and serve on salad plates.

1 container (6 ounces) fat-free Greek yogurt (or use low-fat; optional)

2 tablespoons fat-free cream cheese (or use low-fat; optional)

2 tablespoons pineapple juice

1 can (8 ounces) crushed pineapple, drained

1 medium apple, cored and coarsely chopped

½ cup coarsely chopped walnuts

½ cup coarsely chopped celery (1 large stalk)

½ cup red grapes, halved

1 container (8 ounces) light whipped topping, thawed

Make My Day

I love to serve this salad when I have friends over. It looks great, like you put a lot of work into it, even though you didn't. And since it's made ahead of time, it's one fewer thing you have to worry about on the day you're having folks to your place.

BREAKIN' IT DOWN

	Before	After
Fat	19.5g	7g
Calories	292	144

4g protein | 15g carbohydrate
1g fiber | 53mg sodium

Nutritional count based on 9 servings

SATISFYING SALADS

Caesar Salad

You'll find a Caesar salad on most restaurant menus. And odds are, it will be loaded up with fat. Many Caesar salads can have as many as 300 calories and 27 grams of fat. In a traditional restaurant, this is definitely not the salad you want to choose if you're trying to eat healthfully. Luckily, you can go home and make my version and be guilt free. Just as they do in restaurants, I like to grill up a piece of chicken or some shrimp and throw them on top to make this a complete meal. **Serves 4**

3 cups 1-inch Italian bread cubes

¼ cup light mayonnaise

⅓ cup grated Parmesan cheese

2 tablespoons fresh lemon juice

½ teaspoon Worcestershire sauce

1 garlic clove, finely chopped

¼ teaspoon salt

Freshly ground black pepper to taste

6 cups torn romaine lettuce leaves

1. Preheat the oven to 350°F. Spread the bread cubes on a rimmed baking sheet and lightly spray with cooking spray. Bake about 10 minutes, or until golden.

2. Meanwhile, in a small bowl, whisk together the mayonnaise, Parmesan, lemon juice, Worcestershire sauce, garlic, salt, and pepper.

3. In a large serving bowl, combine the lettuce, bread cubes, and dressing. Toss well to combine.

BREAKIN' IT DOWN

	Before	After
Fat	27g	8g
Calories	300	152

8g protein | 18g carbohydrate
1g fiber | 542mg sodium

Crafty Croutons

Homemade croutons are a much healthier choice than the kind you buy in the supermarket. If you make them yourself, you are in control of the fat and sodium. And they take no time at all to whip up. For an even healthier crouton, use whole-wheat Italian bread instead of white.

Chef's Salad

This recipe has everything I love in a salad. It's packed with protein, cheese, and lots of fresh baby greens and topped off with a creamy, zinging dressing. And you don't have to stick with the same meat and cheese every time you make it. When I don't have turkey breast on hand, I throw some low-sodium boiled ham in there. If I'm out of Swiss, I turn to Cheddar or feta. This is more than just your average salad. It truly is a quick, hearty, and versatile main meal. **Serves 4**

1. To make the dressing: In a small bowl, whisk together the garlic, mustard, vinegar, salt, and pepper. Whisk in the mayonnaise, oil, and 2 tablespoons water.

2. Cut the eggs in half lengthwise. Pop out the yolks and discard, then coarsely chop the whites.

3. In a large bowl, combine the chopped egg whites, baby greens, turkey, tomatoes, cucumbers, Swiss cheese, and avocados. Add the dressing and toss well to combine.

1 garlic clove, finely chopped

2 tablespoons Dijon mustard

1 tablespoon plus 1 teaspoon red wine vinegar

½ teaspoon salt

¼ teaspoon freshly ground black pepper

2 tablespoons fat-free mayonnaise (or use low-fat; optional)

2 tablespoons olive oil

3 large hard-boiled eggs, peeled

10 cups mixed baby greens

4 ounces fat-free smoked turkey breast, sliced into ½-inch strips (about ½ cup)

1 cup cherry tomatoes, halved

1 cup peeled and thinly sliced cucumber

¾ cup finely chopped low-fat Swiss cheese

1 avocado, pitted, peeled, and finely chopped

Dress for Success

To keep salads crunchy, I dress them just before serving. If the dressing goes on too early, the salad will end up limp and soggy. If I'm not sure I'll be finishing the whole salad, I dress each portion as I serve it up. That way I can keep the leftover salad fresh for another meal.

BREAKIN' IT DOWN

	Before	After
Fat	25g	19g
Calories	470	283

18g protein | 12g carbohydrate
5g fiber | 855mg sodium

Black-eyed Pea Salad

This salad is an absolute riot of colors. Once you clap your eyes on it, you just can't wait to dig in. I swapped out the sugar in my Mama's recipe for a splash of OJ and left out most of the oil because with flavor this bold, I didn't really need it. I even added some cheese and still came out ahead. **Makes 6 cups / Serves 8**

2 cans (15½ ounces each) black-eyed peas, rinsed and drained

1 large red bell pepper, finely chopped

1 large yellow bell pepper, finely chopped

4 ounces low-fat pepper Jack cheese, cut into pea-size cubes

½ cup coarsely chopped scallions (white and light green parts only)

¼ cup coarsely chopped fresh parsley

3 tablespoons olive oil

3 tablespoons fresh orange juice

2 tablespoons red wine vinegar

2 tablespoons coarsely chopped fresh oregano

Freshly ground black pepper to taste

In a large bowl, add the black-eyed peas, bell peppers, pepper Jack, scallions, parsley, oil, orange juice, vinegar, oregano, and pepper to taste. Stir to combine. Let the salad sit for about an hour for the flavors to blend. And that's it!

BREAKIN' IT DOWN

	Before	After
Fat	11.5g	8g
Calories	235	190

8g protein | 24g carbohydrate
6g fiber | 330mg sodium

Superior Salad

Because this dish is so easy to throw together and can be made ahead without the worry of it wilting on you, this is the side salad I turn to for most tailgates, picnics, and barbecues. It's a knockout served next to any grilled meat or fish.

Buffalo Chicken Salad

The Buffalo chicken in this salad is crispy, spicy, and sweet. It is so darn good even I have a hard time believing it's good for me. Once you try this salad, you'll never miss those messy Buffalo wings again. **Serves 4**

2 tablespoons hot sauce

1 tablespoon honey

1 tablespoon low-calorie butter substitute spread, melted

¾ pound boneless, skinless chicken thighs, cut into bite-size pieces (about 28 pieces total)

1 teaspoon The Lady's House Seasoning (page 16)

¾ cup panko bread crumbs

1 head Romaine lettuce, torn into pieces (or use a 12-ounce bag)

½ cup blue cheese dressing (see page 39)

1. Preheat the oven to 400°F and position a rack in the upper third of the oven. Spray a rimmed baking sheet with cooking spray.

2. In a medium bowl, combine the hot sauce, honey, and butter substitute. Season the chicken pieces with the House Seasoning and add to the hot sauce mixture, tossing to coat.

3. Place the panko in a deep plate and dredge the chicken, a few pieces at a time, to coat.

4. Arrange the chicken on the prepared baking sheet and bake, turning once, until well browned on both sides, about 15 minutes total.

5. In a large bowl, toss the lettuce with the dressing. Divide the lettuce among four plates and top with the chicken.

BREAKIN' IT DOWN

	Before	After
Fat	49g	8g
Calories	672	270

24g protein | 25g carbohydrate
3g fiber | 844mg sodium

Split It

While I love to cook, even I need a meal out now and again. When I do eat out, I have a few ways to keep the extra calories in check. First and foremost, I skip the bread basket. Additionally, I pass on soft drinks and tend to stick with good clean water. What I've also found helpful is splitting an entrée with a friend. It's a great way to automatically cut my calories in half. Meals in most restaurants tend to be so large these days, and eating a whole entrée only leaves me stuffed. So go ahead and share your next entrée with a friend. You'll also like the effect it has on your bill.

Rotelle Pasta Salad with Garlicky Broccoli and Mozzarella

This Italian-inspired salad looks almost as good as it tastes. It's so colorful on the plate that you just know it's going to taste good, even before you take one bite. The balsamic and garlic provide plenty of bold flavor. Make sure, though, that you chop your garlic good and small so that it doesn't give too much of a bite. **Serves 4 to 6**

6 cups loosely packed broccoli florets

½ cup bottled light balsamic vinaigrette

3 garlic cloves, very finely chopped

6 ounces rotelle pasta

1 cup finely chopped skim mozzarella

½ cup cherry tomatoes, quartered

3 tablespoons coarsely chopped fresh basil

Pinch of crushed red pepper flakes

1. In a large pot of boiling salted water, cook the broccoli until crisp-tender, about 1 minute. Remove the broccoli with a slotted spoon, reserving the cooking liquid in the pot, and spread out the broccoli on a paper towel–lined baking sheet to drain and dry completely. Once dry, toss with the dressing and the garlic in a large serving bowl.

2. Bring the water back up to the boil and add the pasta. Cook according to the package directions. Drain well and cool completely.

3. Add the cooled pasta to the bowl with the broccoli and dressing, along with the mozzarella, tomatoes, basil, and red pepper flakes. Toss to coat and combine.

BREAKIN' IT DOWN

	Before	After
Fat	37g	3g
Calories	612	210

14g protein | 34g carbohydrate
4g fiber | 526mg sodium

Nutritional count based on 5 servings

Keep It Balanced

To avoid calorie and carb overload in pasta salads, I always add more veggies and less pasta. I keep the cheese content down by cutting the mozzarella into smaller pieces. That way I get more cheesy flavor in every bite without the extra calories and fat.

CHAPTER 4

Family Dinner

EATING RIGHT IS NOW A WAY OF LIFE FOR ME. And, for the most part, I stick to a healthy diet. But let me be perfectly honest. I am not one to pass up a classic Sunday supper at my Mama's or brother Jamie's house. There's nothing like sitting around the table with my family sharing a home-cooked meal that was made with all the love we feel for one another. These meals are made with food that is rich in flavor, comforting, and, well, usually on the heavy side.

Fortunately, I've found a way to turn Sunday food into Monday food when I don't want something heavy to weigh me down for the week. Waiting all the workweek for a meal you can look forward to just does not cut it. The best way to eat right is to give yourself good choices that *also* satisfy cravings right through the week.

Take, for instance, my **Charleston Shrimp and Grits** (page 74). Now, my Mama makes just about the best shrimp and grits I have ever come across, but it's a dish best saved for a special weekend dinner. Heavy cream and rich tasso sausage are definitely not Monday foods. You get where I'm going here? I, on the other hand, make my shrimp and grits with fat-free half-and-half and lean Canadian bacon. It's equally delicious, yet only 211 calories and 6 grams of fat per serving.

When we were growing up in Georgia, meat had a starring role in most of our family meals. These days, I try to keep the meat portions smaller and fill out the plate with vegetables, fruit, and whole grains as much as possible. When I'm craving a hearty piece of meat, I turn to **Roasted Pork Tenderloin with Apples** (page 68). I love the way the apples and pork marry so well together. The apples soak up all the meaty pork flavor that I find myself dreaming about so often. Dishes like this will make you forget you're eating your midweek meal.

As an added bonus, all the recipes in this chapter make for great leftovers. And that's important during the week, when time is short. **Sunday Roast Chicken** (page 55), for instance, is the perfect addition to any salad or a great starting point for a chicken salad sandwich. If you're cooking for a family, put two chickens in the oven next time. That way you'll have one for dinner that night and the other for leftovers all week.

Dishes like **Chicken Divan** (page 60) and **Old-fashioned Meat Loaf** (page 66) are the kind of food that brings the whole family running to the table, whether it's Sunday or Tuesday. It's the food you crave, made better for you. But most important, this is the food that satisfies during the week, while still allowing you to splurge on the weekend. My Mama will be so relieved.

Savory Smothered Chicken

The sauce is creamy and rich, and the chicken is absolutely swimming in it. You'd think this was a calorie and fat buster for sure. But at 247 calories and 9 grams of fat, you can feel good about yourself after taking down this meal. I like to pair up this dish with a side of Buttermilk Mashed Potatoes (page 129) so that I can sop up all the creamy gravy with my mash. **Serves 4**

2 tablespoons olive oil

4 boneless, skinless chicken breasts (4 ounces each)

½ teaspoon The Lady's House Seasoning (page 16)

1 Vidalia or other sweet onion, thinly sliced

2 tablespoons all-purpose flour

1 cup low-sodium chicken broth

½ cup 2% evaporated milk

2 tablespoons dry white wine

¼ teaspoon dried thyme

1. In a large skillet, heat the oil over medium-high heat. Season the chicken with ¼ teaspoon of the House Seasoning, add it to the skillet, and cook until golden, about 2 minutes per side. Set the chicken aside on a plate.

2. Add the onions to the skillet, reduce the heat to medium, and cook, stirring frequently, until softened, 7 to 8 minutes. Sprinkle the flour over the onions and stir for a minute to incorporate. Add the chicken broth, evaporated milk, white wine, thyme, and the remaining ¼ teaspoon House Seasoning. Raise the heat to high and bring the mixture to a boil, stirring constantly. Cook until thickened, about 2 minutes.

3. Return the chicken to the skillet, spooning the sauce over the top of the chicken. Cover the skillet, reduce the heat to medium-low, and simmer gently until the chicken is cooked through, about 10 minutes.

BREAKIN' IT DOWN

	Before	After
Fat	**20.5g**	**9g**
Calories	**380**	**247**

28g protein | 14g carbohydrate
.75g fiber | 490mg sodium

Waste Not

Most chicken breasts these days will tend to be a bit larger than 4 ounces, so if you are counting calories and your fillets look big, be sure to trim them down to keep this recipe in balance. But don't toss your trimmings. Save them in the fridge or freezer for your next stir-fry, or add them to your next soup.

Sunday Roast Chicken

If it's Sunday in the South, you can bet most households are prepping up a bird or two for dinner. There's nothing like starting the week with roast chicken and enjoying the leftovers in salads, sandwiches, and just about anything else throughout the week. **Serves 4**

1. Preheat the oven to 400°F. Lightly spray a small roasting pan with cooking spray.

2. In a small bowl, combine the rosemary, paprika, and garlic. Slide this mixture under the skin of the chicken, covering as much meat as possible. Rub the skin all over with the oil and season the chicken inside and out with the salt and pepper. Stuff the lemon pieces inside the chicken's cavity.

3. Place the chicken in the prepared roasting pan and roast until the juices run clear when the chicken is pricked in the thickest part of the thigh, about 1 hour. Once it's cool enough to handle, carve the chicken, removing and discarding the skin as you go.

1 tablespoon finely chopped fresh rosemary

1 teaspoon paprika

3 garlic cloves, finely chopped

1 3-pound chicken, rinsed and patted dry

1 tablespoon olive oil

1 teaspoon salt

¾ teaspoon freshly ground black pepper

1 lemon, quartered

Skip the Skin

Would you believe that half the fat in a chicken can be found in the skin? That, folks, is the reason I remove the skin from my whole chicken after I cook it. However, first cooking the chicken with the skin on does help to lock in all the juices. That's especially important when you are cooking a whole bird, which spends a fair amount of time in the oven and can dry out.

BREAKIN' IT DOWN

	Before	After
Fat	62g	19g
Calories	782.5	349

42g protein | 1.2g carbohydrate
.5g fiber | 703mg sodium

Crispy Oven-Fried Chicken

The key to tender, delicious fried chicken is a good long soak in buttermilk. As it turns out, the same holds true for this roasted version of fried chicken. What you'll end up with is moist, delicious chicken on the inside, with a crunchy, crispy coating. That's exactly what I look for when I'm craving fried chicken. **Serves 4**

⅓ cup 1% buttermilk

¼ cup finely chopped fresh chives

1 teaspoon Dijon mustard

¼ teaspoon hot sauce

4 bone-in chicken breasts (about 12 ounces each)

½ teaspoon salt

½ teaspoon freshly ground black pepper

½ cup dried bread crumbs

1. In a medium bowl, whisk together the buttermilk, chives, mustard, and hot sauce. Remove the skin from the chicken breasts, add the chicken to the bowl, and let it soak for at least 30 minutes or overnight.

2. Preheat the oven to 425°F. Spray a rimmed baking sheet with cooking spray.

3. Remove the chicken from the marinade and season it with salt and pepper. Place the bread crumbs in a wide, shallow bowl. Dip the chicken into the bread crumbs and toss well to coat. Place the chicken on the prepared baking sheet. Spray the chicken generously with cooking spray and bake until it is just cooked through, 25 to 30 minutes.

BREAKIN' IT DOWN

	Before	After
Fat	40g	10g
Calories	797	342

51g protein | 11g carbohydrate
1g fiber | 268mg sodium

Get Cheesy

To make this dish just a little more decadent without adding too many more calories, I like to grate some Parmesan or pecorino Romano into my bread crumbs. About 2 tablespoons should give you a nice cheesy flavor in your crust.

Zesty Chicken Fajitas

I love that all the components of these zesty fajitas sit on a single rimmed baking sheet and spend less than ten minutes under the broiler. So quick, y'all. The orange-chipotle marinade is packed with so much outstanding flavor that you don't really need to top these fajitas with anything. But, if you like, go ahead and top them with some avocado and yogurt (my stand-in for sour cream) for a real Southwestern flavor. **Serves 4**

½ cup fresh orange juice

2 chipotles (from a can of chipotles in adobo sauce), or use just 1 for a milder heat

2 garlic cloves, coarsely chopped

¾ teaspoon salt, plus extra for the vegetables

½ teaspoon freshly ground black pepper

½ teaspoon dried oregano

1 pound boneless, skinless chicken breasts, cut crosswise into ½-inch slices

1 medium onion, cut into thin rounds

2 medium bell peppers (any color you like), cut into strips

4 (8-inch) whole-wheat tortillas

1 avocado, pitted, peeled, and finely chopped, for serving

¼ cup fat-free Greek yogurt (or use low-fat; optional), for serving

1 lime, cut into 8 wedges, for serving

1. Using a blender, food processor, or immersion blender, puree the orange juice, chipotles, garlic, salt, pepper, and oregano until smooth. In a large resealable plastic bag, combine the chicken and the marinade. Refrigerate for at least 30 minutes or overnight.

2. Preheat the broiler. Spray a rimmed baking sheet with cooking spray.

3. Lift the chicken out of the marinade, letting any excess drip off. Arrange the chicken on one half of the prepared baking sheet. Place the onions and peppers on the other side of the baking sheet, season with extra salt, and spray lightly with cooking spray. Broil until the chicken is cooked through and the vegetables are browned in spots, 5 to 7 minutes.

4. Meanwhile, heat a medium cast-iron skillet over medium-high heat. Add the tortillas, one at a time, and warm on both sides, about 10 seconds per side. Serve the chicken and vegetables wrapped in the tortillas. If you like, top with avocado and yogurt and place lime wedges on the side.

BREAKIN' IT DOWN

	Before	After
Fat	27g	2.5g
Calories	572	286

29g protein | 40g carbohydrate
5.5g fiber | 989mg sodium

Let It Marinate

Marinades like the one in this recipe are a great way to pack a dish with flavor without adding a ton of fat and calories. I marinate everything: chicken, meat, fish, and vegetables. Marinades build flavor into my protein, allowing me to cook them simply and practically fat-free.

Chicken Divan

When I've got leftover cooked chicken breast in the fridge, this is the recipe I like to dust off. It's an oldie but a goodie. I just can't walk on by a rich creamy sauce like the one here. It tastes so sinfully delicious, helped along by low-fat sour cream and mushroom soup. And I love the subtly exotic flavor you get with the addition of curry powder. The smell of this luscious dinner cooking away in the oven is sure to bring the family running to the table. Thank goodness it took only a little bit of jiggering to keep this recipe in my rotation. **Serves 4**

1 pound cooked white-meat chicken, cut into cubes (about 1¼ cup)

2 cups cooked and drained broccoli florets

1 can (10¾ ounces) condensed low-fat mushroom soup

½ cup grated low-fat Cheddar cheese

½ cup low-fat sour cream

¼ cup 1% milk

¼ cup dry white wine

½ teaspoon curry powder

¼ cup panko bread crumbs

¼ cup grated Parmesan cheese

1. Preheat the oven to 350°F. Lightly spray a 9-inch square baking pan with cooking spray.

2. In a large bowl, combine the chicken, broccoli, soup, Cheddar, sour cream, milk, white wine, and curry powder. In a small bowl, combine the panko and Parmesan. Scrape the chicken mixture into the prepared pan and top with the panko mixture. Bake for about 30 minutes, or until golden and bubbly.

BREAKIN' IT DOWN

	Before	After
Fat	**41g**	**10g**
Calories	**601**	**327**

36g protein | 18g carbohydrate
2.3g fiber | 829mg sodium

Pick Parmesan

I love Parmesan cheese. When I'm craving a hit of cheese in my food, this is the first cheese I reach for. It's naturally lower in fat than many other cheeses and a fantastic source of protein and calcium. But best of all, Parmesan delivers a concentrated hit of flavor, which means a little goes a long way.

Pot-Roasted Turkey

How easy is this stunning dish? Everything goes into one pot and braises in the oven. This warm, comforting meal will fill your home with the most wonderful aromas of orange, rosemary, and roasting turkey. When just the smell of dinner in the oven sets your mouth watering, you know you've got yourself a family dinner winner. **Serves 6**

1. Preheat the oven to 325°F.

2. In a medium Dutch oven, heat the oil and butter over medium-high heat. Season the turkey all over with salt and pepper and add to the pot. Brown the turkey on all sides, about 8 minutes total, and set on a plate.

3. Add the onions to the pot and cook, stirring frequently, until softened, about 3 minutes. Add the garlic and cook for 30 seconds. Add the chicken broth, orange juice, and rosemary and bring to a boil. Return the turkey to the pot, cover, and bake in the oven for 30 minutes.

4. Stir the squash into the pot, coating it well with all the juices. Cover and continue to bake until an instant-read thermometer inserted into the center of the turkey reads 160°F, another 30 to 45 minutes.

5. Set the turkey on a carving board and tent loosely with foil. Using a slotted spoon, transfer the squash to a bowl and cover with foil.

6. In a small bowl, stir together the cornstarch and 1 tablespoon cold water until the cornstarch is dissolved. Add to the Dutch oven and bring the gravy to a boil over medium-high heat, stirring, until thickened, 1 to 2 minutes. Season the gravy with salt and pepper.

7. Slice the turkey and place on a serving platter with the squash alongside. Pass the gravy in a sauceboat at the table.

1 tablespoon olive oil

1 tablespoon unsalted butter

1 boneless turkey breast (2 pounds), tied

Salt and freshly ground black pepper to taste

1 medium onion, coarsely chopped

1 garlic clove, finely chopped

1 cup low-sodium chicken broth

½ cup fresh orange juice

1 teaspoon coarsely chopped fresh rosemary

1 medium butternut squash, peeled, seeded, and cut into 1-inch chunks (3 cups)

1 tablespoon cornstarch

Subs 'n Swaps

Sometimes I swap out the rosemary in this dish for sage. Turkey and sage is a classic pairing that works well with the earthy butternut squash.

BREAKIN' IT DOWN

	Before	After
Fat	35g	7g
Calories	1,200	244

31g protein | 16g carbohydrate
.7g fiber | 987mg sodium

Turkey Marsala

Apart from during the holiday season, turkey tends to get overlooked during the rest of the year. But I tell you it's a great option for a family meal. Turkey is not only relatively inexpensive, but it is versatile too—whether it's a whole bird, a boneless breast, or lean ground meat. And it's especially suited to quick-cooking recipes like this one. At a cooking time of about two minutes per side, these lean turkey cutlets won't have time to dry out. **Serves 4**

8 ounces white button or cremini mushrooms, halved (larger ones quartered)

Freshly ground black pepper to taste

1 tablespoon olive oil

1 tablespoon unsalted butter

Salt to taste

1 pound thin-cut (about ¼ inch thick) turkey cutlets

¼ cup all-purpose flour

⅓ cup dry marsala

¼ cup low-sodium chicken broth

1. Preheat the oven to 450°F. Spray a rimmed baking sheet with cooking spray.

2. Place the mushrooms on the prepared baking sheet, spray lightly with cooking spray, and season with pepper. Roast, giving the sheet a shake after 5 minutes, until the mushrooms are browned, about 8 minutes.

3. Meanwhile, in a large nonstick skillet, heat the oil and butter over medium-high heat. Season the turkey with salt and pepper. Place the flour in a wide, shallow bowl and dredge the turkey in the flour, shaking off any excess. Working in batches, cook the cutlets, turning once, until golden, about 2 minutes per side. Set on a warm plate.

4. Standing back from the hot skillet, add the marsala and chicken broth. Raise the heat to high and let the sauce reduce by half, about 2 minutes. Stir the mushrooms into the sauce and pour the sauce over the turkey. Serve it up just as soon as you can.

FROM MAMA'S TABLE TO MINE

BREAKIN' IT DOWN

	Before	After
Fat	37g	8g
Calories	770	250

29g protein | 11g carbohydrate
.8g fiber | 85mg sodium

Subs 'n Swaps

Try this recipe with chicken cutlets if that's what you've got on hand. Or, for something a little more decadent, use veal scaloppini.

62

Stick-to-Your-Ribs Chili

Ground sirloin has such great flavor and just enough fat that you don't have to add any extra oil for sautéing the onions and garlic. This is a big, unapologetic chili that still has only about 324 calories per serving. And it just gets better the next day, if it even makes it to the next day! **Makes 12 cups / Serves 8**

1. In a large Dutch oven, cook the beef and onions over medium-high heat, breaking the meat up with a fork, until no pink remains, about 5 minutes. Add the garlic and cook for 30 seconds. Add the kidney beans, tomatoes, chili powder, salt, cumin, and oregano and bring to a boil. Lower the heat, cover, and simmer for 1 hour, stirring occasionally.

2. Add the corn and green beans to the pot, return to a simmer, and cook until the vegetables are tender, about 10 minutes. Serve with dollops of sour cream and a sprinkling of scallions.

2 pounds 95% lean ground sirloin

1½ cups finely chopped onions

2 garlic cloves, finely chopped

2 cans (15½ ounces each) red kidney beans, rinsed and drained

2 cans (14½ ounces each) low-sodium diced tomatoes

3 tablespoons chili powder

1½ teaspoons salt

1 teaspoon ground cumin

1 teaspoon dried oregano

1 package (10 ounces) frozen corn

1 package (10 ounces) frozen green beans

½ cup fat-free sour cream (or use low-fat; optional), for serving

½ cup coarsely chopped scallions (white and light green parts only), for serving

Spicy Option

If you like your chili spicy, try using three cans of Ro-Tel diced tomatoes with chiles in place of the two cans of diced tomatoes. You'll get out-of-this-world Southwest flavor.

BREAKIN' IT DOWN

	Before	After
Fat	38g	6g
Calories	524	324

33g protein | 28g carbohydrate
7g fiber | 489mg sodium

Nutritional count does not include sour cream and scallions for serving

Grilled Filet Mignon with Vidalia Onions

Is there any more perfect way to cook than on the grill? Not in my book. There's something about cooking outside that makes the food taste so much better. And when you start with something like beef tenderloin and Vidalia onion, it's hard to go wrong. For some reason, whenever I throw this on the barbecue at my place in Savannah, friends end up knocking at my door. Just as well. I'm always sure to cook a little extra just in case. **Serves 6**

4 beef tenderloins (6 ounces each, 1½ inches thick)

1 tablespoon finely chopped fresh rosemary

4 teaspoons olive oil

1 garlic clove, finely chopped

1 teaspoon freshly ground black pepper

1 tablespoon Dijon mustard

1½ teaspoons balsamic vinegar

1½ teaspoons honey

1 large Vidalia or other sweet onion, cut into ½-inch-thick slabs

1 teaspoon salt

Metal or presoaked bamboo skewers

1. Toss the tenderloins with the rosemary, 2 teaspoons of the oil, the garlic, and ¾ teaspoon of the pepper. Let stand, covered, for 1 hour at room temperature.

2. Meanwhile, to make the glaze for the onions, whisk together the mustard, vinegar, and honey in a small bowl.

3. Spray the grill grate with cooking spray and preheat the grill to medium-high heat. Thread the onion slabs onto the skewers, piercing each slab with two parallel skewers and leaving about 1 inch of space between each slab. Brush the onions with the remaining 2 teaspoons oil and grill, covered, until almost tender, 4 to 5 minutes per side. Baste both sides with the glaze and grill, covered, for 2 minutes more.

4. Season the tenderloins with the salt and the remaining ¼ teaspoon pepper. Place them on the grill and cook, covered, until you reach the doneness you like, 4 to 5 minutes per side for medium-rare. Let the meat rest for 5 minutes before thinly slicing and serving, topped with onions.

BREAKIN' IT DOWN

	Before	After
Fat	30.5g	24g
Calories	495	335

23g protein | 6g carbohydrate
.5g fiber | 510mg sodium

Keep It Safe

Take extra care when spraying your grill grate with cooking spray. I like to spray it before I've begun preheating the grill as the oil can cause the flame to kick up dangerously.

Old-fashioned Meat Loaf

I've got to admit that I was a little nervous taking on meat loaf because Jamie's wife, Brooke, has darn near perfected it. So all my tastings for this recipe were done in Jamie's kitchen. When I got the approval of these two toughest critics, I knew I had a keeper. A classic accompaniment to meat loaf is a scoop of fluffy mashed potatoes. But when I want something really decadent and down home, I pair this meat loaf with a helping of my Yes You Can Mac and Cheese (page 102). **Serves 4**

Meat loaf

1 pound ground turkey

¾ cup fresh bread crumbs (from 2 slices light whole-wheat bread)

½ cup finely chopped Vidalia or other sweet onions

⅓ cup grated carrot

¼ cup 1% milk

¼ cup tomato sauce

1 large egg, lightly beaten

1 garlic clove, finely chopped

1 tablespoon Worcestershire sauce

¾ teaspoon salt

¼ teaspoon freshly ground black pepper

Topping

2 tablespoons ketchup

2 teaspoons light brown sugar

1 teaspoon yellow mustard

1. Preheat the oven to 375°F. Line a rimmed baking sheet with foil.

2. To make the meat loaf: In a large bowl, combine the turkey, bread crumbs, onions, carrot, milk, tomato sauce, egg, garlic, Worcestershire sauce, salt, and pepper. Mix gently but thoroughly. Mound the meat loaf mixture onto the prepared baking sheet, patting it into a loaf shape with your hands.

3. To make the topping: In a small bowl, combine the ketchup, brown sugar, and mustard. Spoon the topping over the meat loaf, using the back of the spoon to spread it evenly.

4. Bake the meat loaf for about 45 minutes, or until the meat is no longer pink on the inside and is cooked through (165°F on an instant-read thermometer). Let it sit for 5 minutes, then slice and serve.

BREAKIN' IT DOWN

	Before	After
Fat	**45g**	**2g**
Calories	**720**	**216**

32g protein | 15g carbohydrate
2g fiber | 775mg sodium

Hands On

My Mama always says that the best kitchen tools you have are the ones God gave you, and they're right on the ends of your arms! When you really need to get in there and get a good vigorous mix going, use a nice clean pair of hands. That's my advice for mixing up this meat loaf. It's faster and more efficient, not to mention kind of fun.

Roasted Pork Tenderloin with Apples

Pork tenderloin is a staple in my kitchen. Would you believe that tenderloin actually has just about the same amount of calories as skinless chicken breasts? It also has less fat than skinless chicken thighs. And you just can't beat the flavor of pork. Pairing it with apple, sage, and mustard is classic and so fitting on a crisp fall day. **Serves 6**

2 pork tenderloins (1 pound each), patted dry

5 teaspoons olive oil

1 teaspoon salt

Freshly ground black pepper to taste

1½ cups thinly sliced Vidalia or other sweet onions

3 cups cored and thinly sliced Granny Smith apples

1 tablespoon finely chopped fresh sage

3 tablespoons apple juice

Spicy brown mustard, for serving

1. Preheat the oven to 475°F.

2. Heat a large skillet over high heat. Coat the pork with 2 teaspoons of the oil and season it with salt and pepper. Add the pork to the skillet and brown on all sides. Place the pork on an ungreased rimmed baking sheet and roast until the meat is 155°F on an instant-read thermometer, about 15 minutes. Let the meat rest for 5 minutes before slicing.

3. Meanwhile, return the skillet to medium heat and add the remaining 3 teaspoons oil. Stir in the onions and cook until softened, about 5 minutes. Add the apples and a pinch of salt. Cook until soft and tender, 5 to 8 minutes. Stir in the sage, then pour in the apple juice and cook until it evaporates. Spoon the apple-onion mixture over the sliced pork and serve with spicy brown mustard.

BREAKIN' IT DOWN

	Before	After
Fat	13g	7g
Calories	357	242

32g protein | 11g carbohydrate
2g fiber | 469mg sodium

Nutritional count does not include mustard for serving.

Go Granny

Granny Smiths are my go-to cooking apples. They are crisp and firm so they don't go all mushy as soon as the heat hits them. They also have a nice tartness with just a subtle hint of sweetness that works great in a savory dish like this.

Barbecue-Style Pork Chops

All throughout the warm-weather days in Georgia, the grill is my best buddy. Ask anyone who knows me in Savannah and they'll say you're most likely to find me out back by the grill. But even I have to admit that some days just weren't made for grilling outside. Luckily, I've come up with this home run of a recipe for capturing that authentic barbecue flavor in the oven. Now I can enjoy finger-lickin' barbecued pork chops right on through the darkest days of winter. **Serves 4**

1½ cups canned low-sodium crushed tomatoes

¼ cup finely chopped onions

2 tablespoons light brown sugar

2 tablespoons fresh orange juice

1 tablespoon Worcestershire sauce

1 teaspoon dry mustard powder

⅛ teaspoon garlic powder

Salt to taste

Freshly ground black pepper to taste

4 boneless center-cut pork chops (4 ounces each, about ½ inch thick)

1. Preheat the oven to 350°F. Lightly spray a baking dish with cooking spray.

2. In a medium saucepan, combine the tomatoes, onions, brown sugar, orange juice, Worcestershire sauce, mustard powder, and garlic powder over medium-high heat. Bring to a boil and season with a pinch of salt and pepper. Reduce the heat to medium and let simmer for 10 minutes, until thickened. Add pepper if you think the sauce needs it.

3. Meanwhile, heat a large nonstick skillet, lightly coated with cooking spray, over medium-high heat. Season the chops with salt and pepper and cook until golden on both sides, about 1 minute per side. Place the chops in the prepared baking dish and pour the sauce evenly over. Bake for 20 minutes, then serve with plenty of napkins.

BREAKIN' IT DOWN

	Before	After
Fat	27g	8g
Calories	573	228

26g protein | 13g carbohydrate
1g fiber | 316mg sodium

Plate It Up

Here's a great tip for keeping your portion sizes under control. Serve your meals on smaller plates. It sounds so simple, but it really does work. Your plate will look fuller with less food on it. As amazing as it might sound, when your eyes see a full plate, they'll send the message to your stomach that you have enough.

Chicken-Fried Steak with Cream Gravy

A box of corn flakes cereal is a handy thing to have in the house. Corn flakes create a crispy, crunchy crust on just about any meat without the need to deep-fry. With corn flakes as a coating, even chicken-fried steak makes my healthy menu. These steaks are crisped up in the oven and then smothered with creamy, beefy gravy. It's a down-home, affordable meal that is sure to satisfy no matter what side of the Mason-Dixon you might be on. **Serves 4**

1. Preheat the oven to 400°F. Spray a rimmed baking sheet with cooking spray.

2. Pour the flour onto a dinner plate. In a shallow bowl, whisk together the milk, egg, and a few dashes of hot sauce. Place the corn flakes, seasoned with 1 teaspoon of the House Seasoning, on a second dinner plate.

3. Season the steaks with the remaining 1 teaspoon House Seasoning. Dredge them in the flour, patting off any excess, then dip them into the egg mixture, letting any excess drip off. Finally, dredge them in the crushed corn flakes, pressing lightly to help the flakes adhere.

4. Place the steaks on the prepared baking sheet. Spray the tops of the steaks lightly with extra cooking spray. Bake until cooked through, about 15 minutes.

5. Meanwhile, in a small cup, mix the cornstarch with 1 tablespoon of the beef broth and stir until the cornstarch is dissolved. In a small saucepan, combine the cornstarch mixture with the remaining beef broth and the half-and-half. Bring to a boil over medium-high heat, stirring frequently. Let the gravy boil, stirring constantly, until thickened, about 2 minutes. Season generously with pepper and serve the steaks smothered in the gravy.

¼ cup all-purpose flour
¼ cup 1% milk
1 large egg, lightly beaten
Hot sauce to taste
3 cups corn flakes, crushed
2 teaspoons The Lady's House Seasoning (page 16)
4 cube steaks (4 ounces each)
1 tablespoon cornstarch
½ cup low-sodium beef broth
¼ cup fat-free half-and-half (or use low-fat; optional)
Freshly ground black pepper, to taste

Subs 'n Swaps

If you can't get your hands on cube steak, just give top or bottom round steak a good pounding with the spiky side of a meat mallet to make your own homemade version of cube steak.

BREAKIN' IT DOWN

	Before	After
Fat	26g	9g
Calories	562	300

28g protein | 26g carbohydrate
1g fiber | 936mg sodium

Nutritional count does not include hot sauce to taste.

Bobby's Favorite Goulash

When I was growing up, Mama always served me goulash on my birthday. It was my absolute favorite then, and it still is today. Since I love it so much, I can't wait for my birthday to roll around each year to enjoy it. However, I came up with my very own quick, easy, and leaner version that I can enjoy anytime I feel like it—which, I have to admit, is pretty often. My version is full of the same robust tomato and beef flavor that I loved so much as a boy. These days, I top it off with a light and refreshing dollop of Greek yogurt just before digging in. **Serves 4**

¾ pound 95% lean ground beef

1 medium onion, finely chopped

1 medium green bell pepper, finely chopped

1 medium red bell pepper, finely chopped

1 can (14½ ounces) low-sodium diced tomatoes

1 can (8 ounces) tomato sauce

½ cup low-sodium chicken broth

1 tablespoon low-sodium soy sauce

½ teaspoon dried basil

½ teaspoon dried oregano

½ teaspoon garlic powder

⅛ teaspoon cayenne pepper, or to taste

Freshly ground black pepper to taste

1 cup whole-wheat elbow macaroni

3 scallions (white and light green parts only), thinly sliced, for serving

1 container (8 ounces) fat-free Greek yogurt (or use low-fat; optional), for serving

1. Heat a large nonstick pot, lightly coated with cooking spray, over medium-high heat. Add the meat and cook, stirring and breaking it up with a fork, until it loses its pink color, about 2 minutes. Add the onions and bell peppers and cook, stirring frequently, until the vegetables begin to soften, 3 to 5 minutes. Add the tomatoes, tomato sauce, chicken broth, soy sauce, basil, oregano, garlic powder, cayenne, and black pepper to taste, and bring to a boil. Reduce the heat and let simmer, covered, for 20 minutes.

2. Stir in the macaroni and let simmer, covered, stirring occasionally until tender, about 15 minutes. Let stand for 20 minutes before serving, topped with the scallions and a dollop of yogurt.

BREAKIN' IT DOWN

	Before	After
Fat	14g	8g
Calories	437	329

29g protein | 41g carbohydrate
7g fiber | 770mg sodium

Nutritional count does not include scallions and yogurt for serving.

Grilled Salmon with Honey Mustard

I love grilled fish on a hot summer day when I don't feel like standing over a hot grill or stove for too long. It cooks up so quickly and needs only simple flavors to make it shine. This preparation with mustard, soy sauce, and lemon juice is tangy and salty, a perfect complement to the buttery salmon. I cook salmon medium-rare because I find overcooked salmon (or any seafood for that matter) tends to lose its nice texture and takes on a fishy taste. I like to serve this fish with a no-cook side like my Quick Pickled Cucumbers (page 142). Quick cooking, no cleanup, and good for you. Yep, fish on the grill is my kind of meal. **Serves 4**

1. Spray the grill grate with cooking spray and preheat the grill to medium-high heat.

2. In a small bowl, whisk together the mustard, honey, soy sauce, lemon juice, and pepper. Season the salmon lightly with the salt and brush with the glaze.

3. Place the salmon, skin side down, on the grill and cook, covered, until it reaches the doneness you like, 7 to 10 minutes for medium-rare. Do not flip it during cooking or the salmon fillet may break apart. Carefully remove it from the grill and place, skin side down, on a serving platter.

2 tablespoons Dijon mustard

2 tablespoons honey

1 teaspoon low-sodium soy sauce

½ teaspoon fresh lemon juice

¼ teaspoon freshly ground black pepper

1 pound skin-on salmon fillet

¼ teaspoon salt

Go Wild

When you are choosing salmon, I recommend wild over farmed. The flavor of wild-caught fish just can't be beat. And in a clean, simple dish like this, you want that real salmon flavor to take center stage.

BREAKIN' IT DOWN

	Before	After
Fat	31g	15g
Calories	342	273

24g protein | 10g carbohydrate
0g fiber | 340mg sodium

Charleston Shrimp and Grits

They say you can't take the South out of the man. So you don't want to get between me and my grits. Luckily, lightening up this dish didn't hurt it one bit. For starters, I use Canadian bacon, which is less fatty than traditional bacon but still gives you that smoky flavor. And I've done away with the cream to cut down on fat and calories. Rest assured, though, my version is just as creamy and indulgent-tasting as grits ought to be. This dish has gone into high rotation on my weekly menu. **Serves 4**

1 tablespoon olive oil

3 Canadian bacon slices

1 medium onion, finely chopped

1 medium green bell pepper, finely chopped

1 garlic clove, finely chopped

¼ cup dry white wine

1 teaspoon cornstarch

½ cup low-sodium chicken broth

½ cup fat-free half-and-half (or use low-fat; optional)

¾ pound large shrimp, peeled and deveined

¾ cup quick-cooking grits

Chopped scallions (dark green tops only), for serving

1. In a large nonstick skillet, heat the oil over medium heat. Add the bacon, onions, and bell peppers and cook, stirring frequently, until the vegetables are softened, 3 to 5 minutes. Add the garlic and cook for 30 seconds. Add the white wine and let it bubble until it is mostly evaporated, about 1 minute.

2. In a small bowl, combine the cornstarch with 1 tablespoon of the chicken broth and stir until dissolved. Add the remaining broth to the skillet along with the half-and-half and the cornstarch mixture. Bring to a gentle boil and cook, stirring, for 3 minutes, until slightly thickened. Add the shrimp and cook until opaque, about 3 minutes.

3. Meanwhile, cook the grits according to the package directions.

4. Serve the shrimp and sauce over the grits, and top with the scallions.

BREAKIN' IT DOWN

	Before	After
Fat	21.2g	6g
Calories	581	211

19g protein | 21g carbohydrate
1.5g fiber | 650mg sodium

Nutritional count does not include scallion for serving.

Sweet Chili-Glazed Grilled Tuna

Tuna is hands down my favorite fish. I love that it's got such a bold flavor and strong texture that it can stand up to almost anything you throw at it. In this recipe, I throw Sriracha hot sauce at it, and true to form tuna is up to the challenge. I like to serve this delicious grilled fish with steamed white or brown rice and grilled or stir-fried asparagus. **Serves 4**

¼ cup honey

2 tablespoons Sriracha or other chili sauce, or to taste

4 tuna fillets (6 ounces each)

Lime wedges, for serving

1. In a small bowl, make the chili glaze by stirring together the honey and Sriracha.

2. Spray the grill grate with cooking spray and preheat the grill to medium-high heat.

3. Grill the tuna fillets on one side for 3 minutes. Brush the cooked side with some of the chili glaze and turn. Cook for 3 more minutes for medium-rare (for medium, cook 4 minutes on each side). Place the tuna, glazed sides down, on a serving platter and generously brush the tops with extra chili glaze. Serve with the lime wedges.

BREAKIN' IT DOWN

	Before	After
Fat	14g	1.6g
Calories	458	221

39g protein | 9g carbohydrate
0g fiber | 313mg sodium

Chili Choices

While you can use any chili sauce you like in this recipe, I highly recommend you try to get your hands on some Sriracha. A Thai hot chili paste that is both tangy and sweet, Sriracha really packs a punch. You'll find it at specialty or Asian markets.

Memphis Dry Rub Shrimp Skewers

This rub is based on the classic Memphis dry rub for pork or beef ribs. By cutting out the ribs and swapping in plump, fresh shrimp, you go from around 800 calories a serving down to an unbelievable 105 calories per serving, without sacrificing any of that great Memphis flavor. **Serves 4**

1 teaspoon paprika

1 teaspoon light brown sugar

1 teaspoon salt

¾ teaspoon chili powder

¾ teaspoon ground cumin

¾ teaspoon garlic powder

½ teaspoon dried oregano

½ teaspoon freshly ground black pepper

⅛ teaspoon cayenne pepper

1 pound large shrimp, peeled and deveined

2 teaspoons vegetable oil

Metal or presoaked bamboo skewers

1. Spray the grill grate with cooking spray and preheat the grill to medium-high heat.

2. In a small bowl, combine the paprika, brown sugar, salt, chili powder, cumin, garlic powder, oregano, black pepper, and cayenne and mix thoroughly.

3. In a medium bowl, toss the shrimp with the oil. Add the dry rub mixture and toss until the shrimp are evenly coated.

4. Thread the shrimp onto the skewers, piercing each shrimp with two parallel skewers, leaving about 1 inch of space between each shrimp. Grill, turning once or twice, until cooked through, 5 to 6 minutes in total.

BREAKIN' IT DOWN

	Before	After
Fat	65g	3g
Calories	832	105

15g protein | 2g carbohydrate

0g fiber | 781mg sodium

Skewer School

Here are a few tips for using skewers on a hot grill. First off, make sure you soak your skewers for about 20 minutes if you are using the wooden ones. This will prevent them from burning on the open flame. When you are threading shrimp or scallops, thread the seafood on two parallel skewers to prevent it from spinning when you turn it on the grill. Lastly, for even cooking on the skewers, make sure you don't crowd the food you thread onto them.

Peachy BBQ Grouper

We take great pride in our peaches in Georgia, so if you can get your hands on some sweet Georgia peaches, definitely use fresh. But don't limit yourself to this dish during the short but sweet peach season. Canned peaches are a perfectly respectable stand-in. Once you've sampled this fish, you won't want to wait for peach season to roll around to try it again. And if your market doesn't have grouper on hand, other white-meat, firm-textured fish like mahi-mahi or snapper are a fine substitute.

Serves 4

1. Using a blender, food processor, or immersion blender, puree 1 cup of the peaches until smooth. Pour into a medium saucepan and stir in the barbecue sauce. Simmer over medium-low heat for 15 minutes.

2. Spray the grill grate with cooking spray and preheat the grill to medium-high heat.

3. Season the fish with the salt and pepper, brush lightly with the oil, and grill, covered, until opaque, 3 to 4 minutes per side. Generously brush both sides of the fish with the peach barbecue sauce during the last few minutes of cooking time.

4. Set the fish on a serving platter and brush the tops of the fillets with more peach barbecue sauce. Finely chop the remaining ½ cup of peaches and scatter chopped peaches and scallions over the fish. Serve with lime wedges.

1½ cups peeled and pitted fresh or canned peaches, drained if canned

¾ cup bottled low-sodium barbecue sauce

4 grouper fillets (5 ounces each), patted dry

½ teaspoon salt

¼ teaspoon freshly ground black pepper

2 teaspoons canola oil

¼ cup sliced scallions (white and light green parts only), for serving

Lime wedges, for serving

Perfect Pairing

Fish paired with a fresh fruit salsa is a match made in heaven. This is healthy, clean food that is packed with all the nutrients and vitamins that your body needs. Get creative and try other fruits, like mangoes, nectarines, or papayas, in place of the peaches.

BREAKIN' IT DOWN

	Before	After
Fat	16g	7g
Calories	637	212

29g protein | 12g carbohydrate
2g fiber | 430mg sodium

Nutritional count using fresh peaches

FAMILY DINNER

Glazed Scallops with Pineapple Salsa

Summers in Georgia are something truly special. And this dish transports me there every time I eat it. Sweet, spicy, and tangy, all brought together on a delicate, perfectly grilled scallop. I could eat this just about every day in summer. It's not so bad the rest of the year, either. **Serves 4**

Salsa

1 cup finely chopped pineapples

½ cup finely chopped red bell peppers

2 tablespoons finely chopped red onions

2 teaspoons fresh lime juice

2 teaspoons finely chopped jalapeños

Scallops

3 tablespoons honey

1 tablespoon low-sodium soy sauce

1 tablespoon fresh lime juice

1 pound sea scallops, patted dry

Freshly ground black pepper to taste

1. To make the salsa: In a small bowl, stir together the pineapples, bell peppers, red onions, lime juice, and jalapeños.

2. To make the scallops: Spray the grill grate with cooking spray and preheat the grill to medium-high heat.

3. In a small bowl, whisk together the honey, soy sauce, and lime juice. Lightly season the scallops with pepper. Grill directly on the grill grate and uncovered, for 2 minutes. Flip the scallops and brush the tops with the honey mixture. Cover and grill until just opaque, 1 to 2 minutes more. Set the scallops on a plate and spoon the salsa over the top.

BREAKIN' IT DOWN

	Before	After
Fat	5g	4g
Calories	232	178

20g protein | 23g carbohydrate
1g fiber | 173mg sodium

Seafaring

Make sure you use sea scallops, not bay scallops, in this dish. Sea scallops are the bigger scallops. They will stand up to the high heat of the grill much better than their smaller cousins.

CHAPTER 5

Casseroles and One-Dish Meals

IF THERE IS ONE MEAL that can take me back to my childhood in an instant, it has got to be baked spaghetti. I loved it then and I love it now. When I would come home from school and smell that meal cooking away in the stockpot, my mouth would just start watering, y'all. Mama loaded it up with tons of ground beef and topped it off with heaps of Cheddar and Monterey Jack that would come out of the oven positively bubbling over with goodness. It didn't get much better than that. **The Son's Baked Spaghetti (Thanks, Mama!)** (page 87) is every bit as delicious, minus a few calories and grams of fat. Paired with a fresh green salad, it's a perfect midweek one-dish meal.

One-dish meals are tailor-made for the busy workweek, especially dishes like **Slow-Cooked North Carolina–Style Pulled Pork** (page 99). With a meal like this, you can toss all your ingredients into the slow cooker, turn the machine on, leave it to cook, and get on with your day, knowing that dinner is bubbling away at home. Coming back to the smell of this pork is pure heaven.

I think casseroles have gotten a bad reputation for being unhealthy for you. That's a shame. A casserole is really just the sum of its parts. Load it up with good things and it will be good for you. It doesn't have to be all about meat and gooey melted cheese or it can be, just lighter versions! During the week I tend to turn to fish and fowl as a leaner source of protein. That's when I enjoy a casserole like my **Spicy Shrimp and Pasta Casserole** (page 98). It's so good, I find I don't even miss the meat.

And when I'm craving a meaty meal? I can't go past my **Cheeseburger Casserole** (page 85). I keep the oil to a bare minimum, and I use extra-lean beef and low-fat cheese. You'd be amazed by how a few simple steps like that can make a dramatic difference in reducing calories.

You see, the beauty of a casserole is that it's so easy to get together you can pull it off any old day of the week. There is, however, one casserole in this chapter that you may want to save for a special occasion. That casserole is the famous **Low-Country Boil** (page 96). Make this shrimp and sausage dish on a warm day, throw some newspaper over a table, and dig in with your hands. Now that is a one-pot meal that deserves a party.

Beaufort Shrimp Pie

My Mama created this tasty seafood pie in honor of the beautiful town of Beaufort, located on one of South Carolina's Sea Islands. It's filled with plump shrimp and salty bacon brought together in a thick and creamy sauce. This pie is a celebration of Beaufort's venerable shellfish industry, and it always takes me right back to our first days in Savannah, after we moved up from Albany. That's when I discovered all the fresh bounty of the sea. Best of all, because it comes together in the blink of an eye, I enjoy this dish (and all the fond memories it brings back to me) right on through the workweek. **Serves 6**

2 teaspoons olive oil

½ cup finely chopped onions

½ cup finely chopped green bell peppers

2 cups fresh bread crumbs

¾ pound cooked, peeled, and deveined large shrimp

1½ cups 1% milk

2 large eggs, lightly beaten

1 teaspoon Worcestershire sauce

¾ teaspoon The Lady's House Seasoning (page 16)

1 teaspoon hot sauce, or to taste

3 turkey bacon slices, coarsely chopped

1. Preheat the oven to 350°F. Lightly spray a 2-quart casserole with cooking spray.

2. In a medium nonstick skillet, heat the oil over medium heat. Add the onions and bell peppers and cook, stirring occasionally, until softened, 3 to 5 minutes.

3. In the prepared casserole, layer the bread crumbs, followed by the shrimp, and top with the cooked onion mixture.

4. In a medium bowl, whisk together the milk, eggs, Worcestershire sauce, House Seasoning, and hot sauce. Pour the egg mixture over the casserole and top with the bacon. Bake until a knife inserted into the center comes out clean, 45 to 60 minutes. Let the casserole stand for 10 minutes before serving.

BREAKIN' IT DOWN

	Before	After
Fat	25g	7g
Calories	413	285

22g protein | 31g carbohydrate
2g fiber | 727mg sodium

Cheeseburger Casserole

This rich dish features all the things you love in a cheeseburger—meat, cheese, onions, tomatoes, mustard, and pickle—baked together with pasta. Back when my brother and I were young, if we were having pasta, we mostly stuck with elbow macaroni and classic spaghetti. These days there are so many varieties of pasta readily available, I like to branch out and try new kinds as often as possible. I use corkscrew-shaped rotini in this dish because I find it holds the hearty, beefy sauce much better than thin pasta does. **Serves 12**

1. Preheat the oven to 350°F. Spray a 9 by 13-inch baking dish with cooking spray.

2. In a large pot of boiling salted water, cook the pasta according to the package directions and drain well.

3. In a large skillet, heat the oil over medium-low heat. Add the onions and cook until soft, about 5 minutes. Stir in the garlic and cook for 30 seconds. Stir in the beef and cook until browned; season with the salt and pepper. Stir in the tomato paste, then add the tomatoes and mustard. Let the mixture bubble gently until it is slightly thickened, about 2 minutes. Toss the meat mixture with the pasta and spread it into the prepared dish. Top with the Cheddar and bake until the cheese is melted, about 15 minutes. Sprinkle the chopped pickles over the top and serve.

2 cups rotini pasta

2 teaspoons canola oil

1½ cups finely chopped onions

1 garlic clove, finely chopped

1 pound 95% lean ground beef

¾ teaspoon salt

½ teaspoon freshly ground black pepper

2 tablespoons tomato paste

1 can (28 ounces) low-sodium diced tomatoes

2 tablespoons Dijon mustard

2 cups grated low-fat Cheddar cheese

¼ cup coarsely chopped dill pickles

No More Tears

To make quick work of finely chopping onions, I use a little food processor. Coarsely chop the onions, toss them into the food processor, and give the processor a few quick pulses. Just like that, your onion-crying days will be over.

BREAKIN' IT DOWN

	Before	After
Fat	27g	4g
Calories	490	193

21g protein | 21g carbohydrate
2g fiber | 534mg sodium

Shepherd's Pie

Shepherd's pie has got to be the most comfortable of comfort foods. My leaner version features the signature shepherd's pie mashed potato crust baked over a rich stew of ground turkey and vegetables. I like to enjoy this meal on a cold winter night, with some college football playing on the TV. Sounds pretty good, doesn't it, y'all?

Serves 6

1½ pounds Yukon Gold potatoes, peeled and cut into chunks

½ cup skim milk

2 teaspoons unsalted butter

1 teaspoon salt

½ teaspoon freshly ground black pepper

2 teaspoons canola oil

1½ cups finely chopped onions

1 cup finely chopped carrots

1 pound lean ground turkey

1 teaspoon dried rosemary

1½ tablespoons tomato paste

¾ cup low-sodium chicken broth

⅔ cup frozen peas

2 tablespoons coarsely chopped fresh parsley

1. Preheat the oven to 375°F.

2. In a large pot, add the potatoes and cover with cold salted water. Bring to a boil over medium-high heat and cook until the potatoes are tender, about 20 minutes. Drain well and mash with the milk, butter, ½ teaspoon of the salt, and ¼ teaspoon of pepper.

3. Meanwhile, heat the oil in a large skillet over medium-high heat. Cook the onions and carrots until soft, 5 to 10 minutes. Add the turkey and cook, breaking up the meat with a fork, until well browned, 5 to 7 minutes. Season with the rosemary, the remaining ½ teaspoon salt, and ¼ teaspoon pepper. Stir in the tomato paste and chicken broth and let simmer for 5 minutes. Stir in the peas.

4. Scrape the meat mixture into an ungreased 1½-quart baking dish. Top with the mashed potato mixture. Bake for 30 minutes, or until golden. Sprinkle with parsley, season with more pepper if you like, and serve.

BREAKIN' IT DOWN

	Before	After
Fat	25g	4g
Calories	440	223

24g protein | 24g carbohydrate
3g fiber | 482mg sodium

Yukon Do It

If you use Yukon Gold potatoes, you will need less milk and butter to make mashed potatoes than if you use starchy russets. Yukons are naturally creamy and soak up fat less readily.

The Son's Baked Spaghetti (Thanks, Mama!)

I just had to include a shout-out to my Mama on this recipe. As kids, Jamie and I always put baked spaghetti on the top of our dinner wish list. Jamie, especially, could not get enough of this dish, and Mama was only too happy to oblige. There wasn't much I wanted to change in this classic. You'll still find the rich tomato sauce and the angel hair pasta, along with ground beef and bubbling cheese. I just lightened it up around the edges a little by using extra-lean beef and light cheeses. I don't think you can mess too much with success like this. **Serves 10**

1. In a large pot, combine the tomato sauce, tomatoes, chicken broth, onions, garlic, parsley, House Seasoning, Italian seasoning, sugar, and bay leaf. Bring to a boil, then reduce the heat to medium-low and simmer, covered, for 1 hour.

2. In a nonstick skillet, cook the beef over medium-high heat, breaking it up with a fork, until no pink remains. Drain the fat from the skillet and add the meat to the sauce. Simmer for 20 minutes more.

3. Meanwhile, preheat the oven to 350°F.

4. In a large pot of boiling salted water, cook the pasta according to the package directions and drain well.

5. Cover the bottom of a 9 by 13-inch baking dish with a few big spoonfuls of the sauce. Layer half of the pasta on top of the sauce, followed by half of the Cheddar, half of the mozzarella, and more of the sauce. Top with the remaining half of the pasta, followed by the rest of the sauce. Bake for 30 minutes. Top with the remaining half of the Cheddar and mozzarella and continue to bake until melted and bubbly, about 10 minutes.

Ingredients

- 1 can (15 ounces) tomato sauce
- 1 can (14½ ounces) low-sodium diced tomatoes
- 1 cup low-sodium chicken broth
- 1 cup finely chopped onions
- 2 garlic cloves, finely chopped
- ¼ cup coarsely chopped fresh parsley
- 1½ teaspoons The Lady's House Seasoning (page 16)
- 1½ teaspoons Italian seasoning
- 1½ teaspoons sugar
- 1 bay leaf
- 1½ pounds 95% lean ground beef
- 8 ounces angel hair pasta
- 1 cup grated low-fat Cheddar cheese
- 1 cup grated part-skim mozzarella cheese

Subs 'n Swaps

Feel free to swap out the beef here for ground turkey, chicken, or even Italian chicken sausage.

BREAKIN' IT DOWN

	Before	After
Fat	33g	8g
Calories	591	289

25g protein | 28g carbohydrate
3g fiber | 621mg sodium

Chicken Potpie

This is one of those dishes that my Mama does so well. You can imagine how nervous I was to create a leaner, lighter version. What I found out, though, was that it was pretty easy to cut out a good chunk of fat and calories. First off, I had to give the boot to the cream of Cheddar soup, replacing it with low-fat Cheddar cheese and skim milk. Then I used all lean white-meat chicken. Lastly, I cut out the bottom crust and concentrated on giving it a flaky, tasty top crust that would be so good on its own, you wouldn't even miss the bottom crust. In the end, the flavor stayed pretty true to Mama's classic, and I felt a whole lot better about going back for a second piece. **Serves 8**

Filling
- 1 tablespoon canola oil
- 1 cup finely chopped onions
- 1 cup finely chopped carrots
- 1½ tablespoons all-purpose flour
- ¾ cup low-sodium chicken broth
- ½ cup skim milk
- ½ cup low-fat Cheddar cheese
- 1½ cups cooked and coarsely chopped boneless, skinless chicken breast
- 1½ cups frozen peas
- ½ teaspoon celery salt

Pastry
- 1¼ cups all-purpose flour
- ¼ teaspoon salt
- ¼ cup canola oil
- 3 to 5 tablespoons ice-cold water

1. Preheat the oven to 375°F. Lightly spray a 9-inch pie plate with cooking spray.

2. To make the filling: In a large skillet, heat the oil over medium heat. Add the onions and carrots and cook until softened, about 5 minutes. Add the flour and cook, stirring, for 30 seconds. Slowly whisk in the chicken broth and milk. Simmer until slightly thickened, about 5 minutes. Whisk in the Cheddar until melted, then stir in the chicken, peas, and celery salt. Scrape the filling into the prepared pie plate.

3. To make the pastry: In a small bowl, whisk together the flour and salt. Mix in the oil with a fork. Knead in enough water until the crust just holds together. On a lightly floured surface, roll out the dough to a 10-inch circle. Drape the crust over the filling in the pie plate and tuck in the sides. Cut two vents in the top of the crust and bake for about 30 minutes, or until the crust is golden and the filling is bubbling.

BREAKIN' IT DOWN

	Before	After
Fat	30g	10g
Calories	494	239

13g protein | 23g carbohydrate
2g fiber | 244mg sodium

Easy Does It

The secret to a flaky, tender crust is not overworking the dough. Be sure you knead the dough only until the crust just holds together. If you're gonna go to the trouble of making it from scratch, you want to make sure it delivers the goods!

Loaded Lasagna

This is a vegetarian dish that even the most committed meat eater in your house will love. It's no accident I chose mushroom and eggplant for this casserole. These two vegetables are hearty enough to stand in for meat, especially in a rich dish like this one. I actually like to serve this vegetarian lasagna with even more vegetables on the side. Because it feels as hearty as a meat dish, it pairs perfectly with a green salad. **Serves 8 to 10**

8 ounces lasagna noodles

8 ounces white mushrooms, quartered

¾ teaspoon The Lady's House Seasoning (page 16)

1 medium eggplant, peeled and cut into ¼-inch-thick rounds

3 cups low-fat cottage cheese

1 package (10 ounces) frozen spinach, thawed, drained, and squeezed dry

1 package (7 ounces) shredded low-fat Italian cheese blend (1¾ cups)

1 large egg, lightly beaten

1 jar (24 ounces) tomato sauce

1. Preheat the broiler and position a rack 6 inches from the heating unit. Spray two rimmed baking sheets with cooking spray.

2. Place the noodles in a large pot and cover with tap water. Let stand until ready to use.

3. Place the mushrooms on one of the prepared baking sheets, spray lightly with cooking spray, and season with ⅛ teaspoon of the House Seasoning. Broil for 7 to 10 minutes.

4. Place the eggplant on the second baking sheet, spray lightly with cooking spray, and season with ½ teaspoon of the House Seasoning. Broil, turning once, until golden, 3 to 4 minutes per side. Lower the oven temperature to 375°F.

5. Meanwhile, in a medium bowl, combine the cottage cheese, spinach, 1 cup of the Italian cheese blend, the egg, and the remaining ⅛ teaspoon House Seasoning, and mix well.

6. Spray a 9 by 13-inch baking dish lightly with cooking spray and layer one-third of the pasta sauce, half of the noodles, half of the eggplant, half of the cottage cheese mixture, and half of the mushrooms. Repeat the layers, ending with the remaining pasta sauce. Top with the remaining ¾ cup Italian cheese blend. Bake about 40 minutes, or until golden and bubbly.

BREAKIN' IT DOWN

	Before	After
Fat	18g	10g
Calories	492	323

22g protein | 24g carbohydrate
5g fiber | 1002mg sodium

Nutritional count based on 9 servings

Broil with Less Oil

I know some people who have never even turned on their broilers! And that's a shame, because the broiler is a quick way to brown meat and vegetables using very little oil. Next to grilling, I think it's one of the easiest ways to keep the fat count down in your dishes.

Chicken and Dumplings

Chicken and dumplings is my kind of Southern comfort. When I'm craving down-home food, I like to whip up this version. I cook the chicken with the skin and bones so that I wind up with a rich, flavorful gravy that cannot be beat. Just make sure you discard the skin and bones after you've picked the meat off, and be sure you give the gravy a good skim to remove fat. You want to get as much extra flavor as you can with as little extra fat as possible. **Serves 8**

3 pounds bone-in, skin-on chicken breasts

2 cups coarsely chopped onions

¾ cup finely chopped celery

2 bay leaves

1 teaspoon dried thyme

2 quarts low-sodium chicken broth

1¾ cups all-purpose flour

2 teaspoons baking powder

¾ teaspoon salt, plus more as needed

Pinch of cayenne pepper

1 cup skim milk

1 can (10¾ ounces) low-fat, low-sodium cream of chicken soup

Freshly ground black pepper to taste

1. In a large pot, place the chicken, onions, celery, bay leaves, and thyme. Pour in the chicken broth. Bring to a boil over medium-high heat. Reduce the heat to medium-low and simmer until the chicken is tender and starting to fall off the bone, about 45 minutes. Remove the chicken from the pot. Once the chicken is cool enough to handle, pick the meat off the bones and shred into large chunks (discard the skin and bones). Skim off any fat from the surface of the broth and return the broth to the simmer.

2. In a medium bowl, stir together the flour, baking powder, salt, and cayenne. Stir in ¾ cup of the milk until just combined. Drop the dough by tablespoonfuls into the simmering broth. Gently shake the pot (do not stir or the dumplings will fall apart). Cover the pot and simmer over medium-low heat until the dumplings are tender and cooked through, 10 to 15 minutes. Be sure to keep the broth simmering at a gentle pace so that your dumplings don't break apart.

3. Gently whisk the remaining ¼ cup milk into the broth and pour in the cream of chicken soup. Shake the pot gently. Return the chicken meat to the pot and season with salt and black pepper.

BREAKIN' IT DOWN

	Before	After
Fat	**20g**	**6g**
Calories	**432**	**309**

31g protein | 31g carbohydrate
3g fiber | 747mg sodium

Save the Salt

Along with low-fat cream of chicken soups, you can also find cream of chicken soups that are low in sodium, as I've used here. So if salt intake is something you're keeping an eye on, go ahead and choose the low-sodium soup.

Shrimp and Sausage Gumbo Casserole

No Southerner worth his or her salt would serve gumbo without rice. So I thought, why not cook the rice right in my gumbo for an easy, complete meal? Brown rice is perfect for this dish. Its nutty flavor and hearty texture stand up nicely next to the assertive Cajun flavors. **Serves 4**

1. Preheat the oven to 350°F.

2. In a medium ovenproof Dutch oven, heat the oil over medium heat. Add the onions, bell peppers, and celery and cook, stirring frequently, until the onions and bell peppers are softened, 3 to 5 minutes. Add the sausage, chicken broth, okra, clam juice, Cajun seasoning, and bay leaf. Bring to a boil, stir in the rice, cover, and bake for 45 minutes.

3. Stir in the shrimp, cover again, and bake for another 15 minutes, until the shrimp are cooked through and the rice is tender.

1 tablespoon olive oil

1 cup finely chopped onions

1 cup finely chopped red bell peppers

1 cup finely chopped celery

¼ pound turkey andouille or other smoked sausage, cut into ¼-inch rounds

3 cups low-sodium chicken broth

1 cup sliced fresh or frozen okra, thawed if frozen

½ cup clam juice

1 teaspoon Cajun seasoning

1 bay leaf

1 cup brown rice

⅓ pound large shrimp, peeled and deveined

Easy Bake

You'll find most traditional gumbos are cooked on the stove top. They generally need a fair bit of tending to and stirring. Not this easy gumbo. It's baked, so there's no need to stand over it as it does its magic.

BREAKIN' IT DOWN

	Before	After
Fat	32g	8g
Calories	563	316

14g protein | 47g carbohydrate
5g fiber | 775mg sodium

Mexican Fiesta Casserole

My invites to tailgate parties usually come with a condition. I absolutely have to show up with this casserole in hand. Since I can whip it up in about twenty minutes flat using only a skillet and a baking dish, this is one condition I'm only too happy to comply with. Most of the time I make it with lean ground turkey. But you can also swap out the turkey and use lean ground beef. This cheesy baked casserole is packed with Mexican flavor, from the spice of the taco seasoning and tomato salsa right on down to the creamy black beans and sweet corn tortillas. It's seriously tasty, seriously easy, and seriously, it's good for you. **Serves 8**

2 teaspoons canola oil

½ pound lean ground turkey

1 cup finely chopped onions

1 cup finely chopped zucchini

1 envelope (1¼ ounces) low-sodium taco seasoning

⅔ cup frozen corn kernels

1 cup canned black beans, rinsed and drained

2 cups jarred salsa

8 (6-inch) corn tortillas

1½ cups shredded reduced-fat Mexican cheese blend

¼ cup sliced scallions (white and light green parts only)

½ cup fat-free sour cream (or use low-fat; optional), for serving

1. Preheat the oven to 350°F. Spray a 9 by 13-inch baking dish with cooking spray.

2. In a large skillet, heat the oil over medium-high heat. Add the turkey and cook until browned, 5 to 7 minutes. Stir in the onions and zucchini and cook until tender, about 5 minutes. Stir in the taco seasoning, ⅔ cup water, and the corn. Simmer until thickened, about 2 minutes, then stir in the black beans.

3. Spread ½ cup of the salsa in the bottom of the baking dish. Lay 4 tortillas over the salsa, and spoon half of the meat mixture on top. Cover with ¾ cup of the salsa and 1 cup of the shredded cheese. Top with 4 more tortillas and add the rest of the meat mixture. Cover with the remaining ¾ cup salsa. Scatter the remaining ½ cup shredded cheese over the top.

4. Bake the casserole until the cheese is melted and bubbling, about 25 minutes. Slice and serve, topped with scallions and sour cream.

BREAKIN' IT DOWN

	Before	After
Fat	23g	6g
Calories	384	236

17g protein | 28g carbohydrate
4g fiber | 858mg sodium

Nutritional count does not include sour cream for serving.

Go Green

This is one of those dishes where you can sneak in your greens, making it great for kids. The zucchini in this casserole takes on all the great Mexican flavors so kids won't even know they're eating something that's good for them. I like to experiment with other vegetables too. Yellow squash, peas, and cut green beans are equally tasty in place of zucchini.

Low-Country Boil

Well hello, party in a pot! This is classic Carolina cuisine all the way. If you've got a big old pot and a heat source, you've got yourself the right place to enjoy a Low-Country boil. I can whip up this smoky, spicy one-pot meal just about anywhere, to the delight and amazement of all. **Serves 4**

2 tablespoons crab boil

¾ **pound small red new potatoes**

½ **pound cooked spicy chicken sausage, cut into 2-inch pieces**

2 **ears shucked fresh corn on the cob, cut in half cross-wise**

1½ **pounds unpeeled large shrimp**

Fill a large pot with 3 quarts water and stir in the crab boil. Bring the liquid to a boil over medium-high heat. Stir in the potatoes and sausage and cook over medium heat until the potatoes are almost tender, about 20 minutes. Stir in the corn and cook for 10 minutes more. Add the shrimp and cook until the shrimp are just opaque, 2 to 3 minutes. Drain well and enjoy.

BREAKIN' IT DOWN

	Before	After
Fat	32g	3g
Calories	684	236

29g protein | 24g carbohydrate
3g fiber

Shrimp and Sausage

A Low-Country boil just about always features shrimp and sausage. If you like, though, you can switch out the shrimp for crab or go ahead and use both. I swap out fatty pork sausage for leaner chicken sausage, but I make sure it's spicy. Low-Country boil absolutely has to have a kick.

Monday-Night Red Beans and Rice

Turkey andouille provides a fair amount of spice, so no need to add hot sauce while cooking this dish. But by all means, pass the hot sauce bottle at the table if you like your beans and rice in true Southern style. **Serves 6**

1. In a medium pot, heat the oil over medium-high heat. Add the sausage, onions, and bell peppers and cook, stirring frequently, until the vegetables are softened, 3 to 5 minutes. Add the garlic and cook for 30 seconds. Add the beans, chicken broth, cumin, thyme, bay leaf, and pepper to taste and bring to a boil. Cover, reduce the heat to medium-low, and simmer for 10 minutes.

2. Serve the beans over the rice, sprinkled with the scallions.

1 tablespoon olive oil

½ pound turkey andouille or other smoked sausage, coarsely chopped

1 medium onion, finely chopped

1 medium green bell pepper, finely chopped

1 garlic clove, finely chopped

2 cans (15½ ounces each) red kidney beans, rinsed and drained

½ cup low-sodium chicken broth

½ teaspoon ground cumin

½ teaspoon dried thyme

1 bay leaf

Freshly ground black pepper to taste

3 cups cooked white rice

Chopped scallions (white and green parts only), for serving

Subs 'n Swaps

As an even healthier alternative, serve these red beans on brown rice. Or, for something a little more exotic tasting, try this dish with a brown and wild rice mix.

BREAKIN' IT DOWN

	Before	After
Fat	24g	10g
Calories	486	273

9g protein | 36g carbohydrate
5g fiber | 537mg sodium

CASSEROLES AND ONE-DISH MEALS

97

Spicy Shrimp and Pasta Casserole

When I'm home in Savannah, I cannot get enough of the out-of-this-world shrimp that's in local abundance. That's why I've got about a million ways to prepare it. This is one of my favorites, ranked right up there with simply boiling the shrimp and popping them right out of their shells and into my mouth. In this hearty layered dish, a dash of Italian seasoning and a nice dose of feta bring out the flavors of the Mediterranean. **Serves 8**

4 ounces whole-grain angel hair pasta

1¼ cups fat-free half-and-half (or use low-fat; optional)

¾ cup fat-free Greek yogurt (or use low-fat; optional)

1 large egg

1 large egg white

2 teaspoons dried Italian seasoning

Pinch of crushed red pepper flakes

1¼ cups grated low-fat Monterey Jack cheese

⅓ cup crumbled low-fat feta cheese

1½ pounds medium shrimp, peeled and deveined

1¾ cups jarred salsa, drained

¼ cup coarsely chopped fresh parsley

1. Preheat the oven to 350°F. Spray a 9-inch square baking pan with cooking spray.

2. Break the pasta into 3-inch pieces. In a large pot of boiling salted water, cook the pasta 1 minute less than the package directions suggest. Drain well.

3. In a large bowl, whisk together the half-and-half, yogurt, egg, egg white, Italian seasoning, and red pepper flakes. Whisk in 1 cup of the Monterey Jack and the feta.

4. Spread half of the pasta into the bottom of the pan. Top with half of the shrimp, all of the salsa, and the remaining ¼ cup Monterey Jack. Finish with the remaining pasta and shrimp and pour in the egg mixture. Bake for about 30 minutes, or until bubbly. Place under the broiler until golden, 2 to 4 minutes. Let stand for 10 minutes. Sprinkle with parsley and serve.

BREAKIN' IT DOWN

	Before	After
Fat	15g	6g
Calories	412	256

30g protein | 15g carbohydrate
2g fiber | 646mg sodium

Pasta Pantry

You'll always find a variety of pastas in my pantry, from angel hair to rotelle to orzo. As my brother, Jamie, likes to say, "If you've got pasta in your pantry, you've got dinner halfway made." And in recent years, I've branched out to the whole-grain pastas now available on supermarket shelves.

Slow-Cooked North Carolina–Style Pulled Pork

Being able to enjoy this slow-cooked pulled pork during the week is such a treat. Without a slow cooker, it would be darn near impossible to fit this into my busy schedule. While it's great for a party, I like to make a big batch, even if I don't have a crowd coming by. That way I've got plenty left over to use in sandwiches, wraps, salads, and whatever else may strike my fancy. **Serves 14 to 16**

1. In a large bowl, stir together the salt, garlic powder, and black pepper. Add the meat and rub the mixture all over the pork. Cover with plastic wrap and refrigerate for at least 3 hours or overnight.

2. In a small saucepan, combine the vinegar, ketchup, brown sugar, Worcestershire sauce, mustard powder, chili powder, and cayenne. Simmer over low heat for 5 minutes.

3. Place the pork in a slow cooker. Pour over two-thirds of the vinegar mixture. Cook until the meat is falling-apart tender, 7 to 8 hours on low heat or 4 to 5 hours on high.

4. Remove the pork from the cooker and place on a rack with a rimmed baking sheet placed underneath. Let stand until cool enough to handle.

5. Meanwhile, in a small saucepan, warm the remaining vinegar mixture over low heat. Place the warm pork on a cutting board and shred or chop the meat into bite-size pieces, discarding any fat or skin. Place the pork in a large bowl, add the sauce to taste, and mix well.

- 2 teaspoons salt
- 1 teaspoon garlic powder
- 1 teaspoon freshly ground black pepper
- 1 boneless pork shoulder (5 pounds), patted dry
- 2 cups apple cider vinegar
- ⅔ cup ketchup
- 2 tablespoons dark brown sugar
- 2 tablespoons Worcestershire sauce
- 1½ tablespoons dry mustard powder
- 1 tablespoon chili powder
- ¼ teaspoon cayenne pepper

It's a Wrap

I like to serve this pulled pork wrapped in big, crisp butter lettuce leaves. The crunchy lettuce balances nicely with the soft, tender pork filling. It's a great low-carb dinner that's just as fun to assemble as it is to eat.

BREAKIN' IT DOWN

	Before	After
Fat	23g	5g
Calories	337	216

34g protein | 7g carbohydrate
0g fiber | 417mg sodium

Nutritional count based on 15 servings

Jambalaya, Y'all

Mama always made jambalaya in the blink of an eye: everything in the pot and no oil needed. Dinner served. That's just the way I like to do it. And with all the tasty Cajun spices thrown into this pot, you can be sure it's hopping with flavor. **Serves 4**

2½ cups low-sodium chicken broth

1 cup long-grain white rice

¾ pound boneless, skinless chicken breasts, cut into 1½-inch pieces

¼ pound smoked turkey sausage, like andouille or kielbasa, sliced

1 can (14½ ounces) low-sodium diced tomatoes

3 tablespoons dried minced onions

1 tablespoon chopped fresh parsley

½ teaspoon dried thyme

½ teaspoon garlic powder

½ teaspoon freshly ground black pepper

⅛ teaspoon cayenne pepper

1 bay leaf

In a Dutch oven, combine the chicken broth, rice, chicken, sausage, tomatoes, onions, parsley, thyme, garlic powder, black pepper, cayenne, and bay leaf. Bring to a boil over medium-high heat. Make sure that all of the rice is submerged in liquid and cover the pot. Reduce the heat to medium-low and simmer, stirring occasionally, until the rice is tender, about 30 minutes.

BREAKIN' IT DOWN

	Before	After
Fat	15g	4g
Calories	445	326

25g protein | 46g carbohydrate
3g fiber | 640mg sodium

Subs 'n Swaps

When I've got a hankering for seafood, I sometimes swap out the chicken for some plump and tasty shrimp. I just add the peeled and deveined shrimp to the pot during the last 5 to 7 minutes of cooking time. Delicious.

Yes You Can Mac and Cheese

Low-fat mac and cheese; sounds like a fantasy, doesn't it? Well, it's not, and this slimmed-down version delivers the goods on taste and texture. You'll get plenty of creamy, cheesy goodness in this one-dish meal. In fact, the only thing missing here is the extra fat and calories. **Serves 8**

4 cups whole-grain elbow macaroni

2 tablespoons unsalted butter

2 tablespoons all-purpose flour

2 cups skim milk

1 cup grated low-fat Cheddar cheese

¼ cup grated Parmesan cheese

2 ounces low-fat cream cheese (Neufchâtel)

½ teaspoon Worcestershire sauce

½ teaspoon dry mustard powder

Freshly ground black pepper to taste

1. In a large pot of boiling salted water, cook the pasta 1 minute less than the package directions suggest. Drain well.

2. Return the pasta pot to the stove and melt the butter in the pot over medium-high heat. Whisk in the flour and cook for 1 minute. Slowly whisk in the milk and simmer until bubbling and slightly thick. Whisk in the Cheddar, Parmesan, cream cheese, Worcestershire sauce, mustard powder, and pepper to taste.

3. Stir the pasta back into the pot and cook until heated through, about 1 minute. Season with some more salt and pepper and serve.

BREAKIN' IT DOWN

	Before	After
Fat	30g	7g
Calories	584	293

15g protein | 45g carbohydrate
4g fiber | 199mg sodium

Pimiento, Please

This mac's got all the makings of my classic pimiento cheese, so why not add some chopped pimiento if you've got some on hand? The pimiento adds a nice tangy note and an eye-catching pop of color.

CHAPTER 6

Sandwiches with All the Fixin's

MY FAMILY OWES A GREAT DEBT to the humble sandwich. As the undeniable star of my Mama's first food business, The Bag Lady, the sandwich set us on an unbelievable journey in the food world that continues to amaze me to this day. Who knew that when Jamie and I were running all over Savannah delivering tasty bag lunches, that tiny business would grow into the hugely popular restaurant it is today. So, as you can imagine, I never take a sandwich for granted.

For my family, a sandwich never meant a plain old slice of turkey with mayonnaise (although I wouldn't knock that in a pinch). Oh no, for the Deens, building the better sandwich is well and truly a competitive art. You're adding peppers to your sandwich? I will do you one better and add some roasted chile to mine. You're heaping some salad onto that sandwich? Look out, I've just piled some quick Southern slaw on mine. Sandwich building is serious business, folks, and less is most definitely not more. That's why my sandwiches have names like **Overstuffed Dagwood Sandwiches** (page 106) and **Bobby's Turkey and Cheese Power Wrap** (page 109). They are a meal, y'all! That's just good sense and good for you, because, if your sandwich is packed with flavor, you're going to feel more satisfied. And when you're satisfied, that means less picking at the chips on the side.

Spending so much time recently in New York working on my TV show, I've been inspired by the sandwich culture there. New York is such a fast city that the sandwich is the perfect way to get a meal in and still stay on the go. I love that it's a meal that I can eat standing up. In a tip of my hat to New York, I've taken a crack at the ultimate New York indulgence sandwich, and I've made it healthier. Once you've tried my **Crispy, Crunchy Reubens** (page 108), you may never go back to the traditional Reuben. The secret is light rye crispbread in place of rye bread.

When I've got leftover chicken in the fridge, I turn to my **Chicken Salad with a Twist** (page 117). I absolutely refuse to throw away leftovers. I just can't do it. I've always got some in the fridge because I cook up a storm on weekends so that I'm stocked for the workweek.

For days when I need a little something extra, something a little more comfort food feeling, there's nothing like my hot **Cajun Sliders** (page 114) to fill me up and warm my insides. I don't make them just for lunch. They're a great, fast dinner option for those busy nights I just don't have time to pull together a proper sit-down meal.

Come to think of it, I'd say sandwiches are just about the most American of meals, equally loved by Southerners and New Yorkers. Now that's saying something.

Overstuffed Dagwood Sandwiches

I'm not afraid to admit it. Sometimes I just need a big sandwich. I like to bring out a platter of these bad boys on game night, with sporty toothpicks to hold them together. Start 'em off with some Fiery Queso Fundido (page 12) and a bucket of beers, and your friends won't want to watch the game any other way. **Makes 8 sandwiches**

⅓ cup fat-free mayonnaise (or use low-fat; optional)

2 tablespoons Dijon mustard

16 slices light whole-wheat bread, toasted

8 ounces sliced smoked turkey

8 dill pickle spears, each cut in half lengthwise

4 ounces thinly sliced ham

8 romaine lettuce leaves, cut so each leaf is a bit wider than the bread

4 ounces thinly sliced roast beef

2 tomatoes, sliced into 4 rounds

8 slices low-fat Swiss cheese

½ cup pickled yellow pepper rings

1. In a small bowl, stir together the mayonnaise and mustard. Spread one side of each slice of toast with the mixture.

2. Divide the turkey, pickles, ham, lettuce, roast beef, tomatoes, cheese, and peppers in the order listed among 8 slices of bread. Top with the remaining slices of bread and secure with a toothpick.

BREAKIN' IT DOWN

	Before	After
Fat	70g	9g
Calories	1,000	326

25g protein | 43g carbohydrate
14g fiber | 1700mg sodium

Slice Your Sodium

You'll find that most deli meat brands offer a low-sodium version of their meat. Good to know if you're a meat lover like me but you're also watching your salt intake.

Crispy, Crunchy Reubens

A lighter, leaner Reuben? Yes, indeed, folks; this is it. But this hot open-face sandwich doesn't just work with Reuben fixings. It works great with pretty much any deli meat and cheese combo. So get creative with what you pile onto this sandwich. Just be sure you don't miss out on my version of Thousand Island dressing. It's the star of this show. **Serves 1/ Makes 1 cup dressing**

Bobby's Best Thousand Island Dressing

½ **cup fat-free Greek yogurt (or use low-fat; optional)**

¼ **cup ketchup**

2 **tablespoons light mayonnaise**

1 **tablespoon sweet pickle relish**

Reuben

2 **slices turkey pastrami (1 ounce each)**

1 **slice light rye crispbread**

1 **tablespoon packaged sauerkraut**

1 **slice low-fat Swiss cheese**

1 **tablespoon Bobby's Best Thousand Island Dressing**

1. To make the Thousand Island dressing: In a small bowl, stir together the yogurt, ketchup, mayonnaise, and pickle relish until combined.

2. To assemble the Reuben: Stack the pastrami onto the crispbread, followed by the sauerkraut and cheese. Place the stack on a microwave-safe plate and heat in the microwave until the cheese is melted, about 20 seconds. Drizzle with 1 tablespoon of the dressing and enjoy. (Save the remaining dressing for another use; see below.)

BREAKIN' IT DOWN

	Before	After
Fat	70g	4.5g
Calories	900	168

20g protein | 12g carbohydrate
2g fiber | 833mg sodium

A Thousand Uses Dressing

Thousand Island dressing is one of my favorites. I love it mixed through a seafood pasta salad, slathered on a nice juicy burger, or drizzled over a simple green salad. It tastes good on just about anything, and that's why I always make more than I need for just one recipe.

Bobby's Turkey and Cheese Power Wrap

This is the on-the-go lunch that I make time for on my way to the gym. It's superlight, yet delicious and satisfying. I can roll one of these up in no time flat and be out the door and on my way, power wrap in hand. **Serves 4**

1. In a small bowl, whisk together the cream cheese and mustard until smooth. Spread the mixture on one side of each wrap. Arrange the turkey over the wraps and scatter the cheese and spinach on top. Sprinkle the avocados and chopped tomatoes over the cheese.

2. Starting at one end, roll the wraps up over the filling, tucking in the sides as you go. Slice each wrap crosswise into four pinwheels and secure each with a toothpick, if you like.

2 tablespoons low-fat cream cheese (Neufchâtel), softened

2 tablespoons Dijon mustard

2 (10-inch) multigrain wraps

5 ounces thinly sliced smoked turkey

⅔ cup grated low-fat Swiss cheese

1 cup baby spinach

½ avocado, pitted, peeled, and finely chopped

⅓ cup finely chopped tomatoes

BREAKIN' IT DOWN

	Before	After
Fat	28g	14g
Calories	457	281

17g protein | 23g carbohydrate
6g fiber | 1,005mg sodium

Avocado BLT

Dialing back the classic BLT is pretty tricky. Two of the great things about a BLT are the crispy pork bacon and the creamy, fatty mayonnaise. That's why I like to add avocado instead. By taking out the fat I'd be getting from the bacon and mayonnaise, I've made room for the good fat found in avocado, not to mention the vitamins and potassium that it's chock-full of. And the avocado's creamy texture, paired with the crunch of the turkey bacon and the tomato, knock this sandwich right out of the park. **Serves 4**

8 turkey bacon slices

¼ cup light mayonnaise

1 tablespoon honey mustard

8 slices whole-wheat bread, toasted

1 medium tomato, thinly sliced

1 avocado, pitted, peeled, and thinly sliced

1 cup mixed greens

1. In a large skillet, cook the bacon over medium-low heat until crisp, 5 to 10 minutes. Set the bacon on a paper towel–lined plate to drain.

2. Whisk together the mayonnaise and honey mustard. Spread one side of each slice of toast with this mixture. Sandwich the bacon, tomatoes, avocados, and mixed greens between bread slices.

BREAKIN' IT DOWN

	Before	After
Fat	40g	17g
Calories	480	334

15g protein | 33g carbohydrate
7g fiber | 875mg sodium

Talking Turkey

The microwave is a really quick, no-mess way to cook turkey bacon. You can get a nice crisp on it and it won't end up rubbery. What you do is place the bacon on a plate, cover it with a paper towel, and cook each side for 1 to 2 minutes. Then just let it cool a minute. As it cools, it will come to an ideal crunchiness.

Southern Tomato Sandwiches

Tomato sandwiches are something special in the South. You'll find them at most afternoon get-togethers, from weddings to birthday parties to christenings. But since they're so easy to make, you'll also find them on the table on any given weekday. Fresh tomatoes paired with Vidalia onions—well, it just doesn't get much more Georgia sweet than that. **Serves 4**

½ cup light mayonnaise

2 tablespoons coarsely chopped fresh basil

½ teaspoon freshly ground black pepper, plus more to taste

8 slices whole-wheat or white bread, crusts removed

2 medium tomatoes, thinly sliced

1 small Vidalia or other sweet onion

1. In a small bowl, whisk together the mayonnaise, basil, and pepper. Spread one side of each slice of bread with the mayonnaise mixture. Top 4 slices of bread with tomatoes and season lightly with pepper.

2. Thinly slice one-half of the onion into rounds, reserving the other half for another use. Top the tomatoes with the onion rings. Cover with the remaining bread slices and serve.

BREAKIN' IT DOWN

	Before	After
Fat	17g	7g
Calories	323	151

3g protein | 20g carbohydrate
3g fiber | 323mg sodium

Nutritional count using whole-wheat bread

Blackened Catfish Po'boys

I try to get down to New Orleans at least once every year. And when I do, you're sure to find me enjoying a po'boy. But when I can't get down to the Big Easy, I make this little beauty of a sandwich right at home. **Serves 4**

1. To make the tartar sauce: In a small bowl, whisk together the mayonnaise, pickles, onions, and pepper.

2. To make the po'boys: Heat a large cast-iron skillet over medium-high heat and spray lightly with cooking spray. Season the catfish with the salt, cayenne, and garlic powder. Place the fish in the skillet and cook, turning once halfway through, until the fish is just flaky, about 4 minutes per side.

3. Spread the tartar sauce on the inside of each portion of bread. Fill with the fish, tomato slices, and lettuce.

Tartar Sauce

¼ cup light mayonnaise

2 tablespoons finely chopped low-sodium dill pickles

2 tablespoons grated onions

Freshly ground black pepper to taste

Po'boys

½ pound catfish fillet, portioned into 4 fillets

¼ teaspoon salt

⅛ teaspoon cayenne pepper

⅛ teaspoon garlic powder

1 baguette (10 ounces), cut into 4 portions and split

1 small tomato, thinly sliced

½ cup coarsely chopped iceberg lettuce

Iron Clad

I always use a cast-iron skillet when I cook fish. It's especially important when I'm cooking blackened fish and I'm using only a small amount of oil. You see, the trick with blackened fish is to get your pan real hot so that the fish doesn't stick and it cooks quickly, and for that, no other pan trumps the cast-iron skillet.

BREAKIN' IT DOWN

	Before	After
Fat	27g	9g
Calories	615	350

22g protein | 45g carbohydrate
2g fiber | 833mg sodium

Cajun Sliders

These sliders bring me right back down South every time I make them. Just jumping with that famous Cajun flavor mix of garlic, bell peppers, oregano, and thyme and spiced with good Louisiana hot sauce, these sliders are not for the faint of heart. If spice is not your thing, though, feel free to skip or reduce the hot sauce in the spread. These mini sandwiches will still make you feel like you took a detour to the Bayou on your lunch break. **Serves 4**

6 ounces 93% lean ground turkey

6 ounces 95% lean ground beef

1 tablespoon ketchup

1 teaspoon Worcestershire sauce

½ teaspoon Cajun seasoning, plus extra for the vegetables

¼ teaspoon hot sauce

½ red bell pepper, cut lengthwise into 8 strips

4 round onion slices (from 1 small onion)

1 tablespoon plus 1 teaspoon fat-free mayonnaise (or use low-fat; optional)

2 teaspoons spicy brown mustard

4 small sandwich buns

1. Preheat the broiler. Spray a rimmed baking sheet with cooking spray.

2. In a medium bowl, combine the turkey, beef, ketchup, Worcestershire sauce, ½ teaspoon Cajun seasoning, and the hot sauce. Form the mixture into 4 fat patties (a little wider than the buns).

3. Spray a large nonstick skillet with cooking spray and place over medium heat. Cook the patties, covered, turning once, until the internal temperature reaches 165°F on an instant-read thermometer, 8 to 10 minutes total.

4. Meanwhile, place the bell pepper strips and onion slices on the prepared baking sheet. Season with a pinch of the extra Cajun seasoning and lightly spray with cooking spray. Broil, without turning, until browned along the edges, 3 to 5 minutes.

5. In a small bowl, stir together the mayonnaise and mustard and spread on the inside of each bun. Put a patty on the bottom of each bun, top with an onion slice and 2 strips of bell pepper crossed over each other, and cover with the top bun.

BREAKIN' IT DOWN

	Before	After
Fat	15g	4g
Calories	310	272

21g protein | 28g carbohydrate
3g fiber | 419mg sodium

The Spice of Life

While the Cajun seasoning in these sliders does add a bit of sodium to your dish, it is also a sensational diet aid. I'm not kidding, folks! When you add bold flavors like this to your dishes, you'll feel more satisfied after eating. A concentrated hit of flavor is a great way to make sure that you don't keep going back for more.

Open-Face Elvis Sandwiches

Elvis Presley brought us this decadent delight, and I just couldn't resist creating my own slimmed-down version. The sweet and creamy peanut butter and banana are heaven when paired with crispy, salty bacon. My nephews and I like to enjoy this sandwich with an ice-cold glass of milk. **Serves 4**

4 slices light stone-ground whole-wheat bread

¼ cup low-fat creamy peanut butter

2 small bananas, thinly sliced

2 bacon slices, cooked and crumbled

2 teaspoons light brown sugar

1. Preheat the broiler and position a rack in the top of the oven.

2. Spread each slice of bread with peanut butter and top with banana slices. Sprinkle the bacon and brown sugar over the bananas.

3. Place the bread slices on a rimmed baking sheet. Broil until the sugar is golden and the bread is lightly toasted, 1 to 2 minutes (watch carefully to see that the bread does not burn).

BREAKIN' IT DOWN

	Before	After
Fat	**23g**	**8g**
Calories	**336**	**245**

10g protein | 39g carbohydrate
7g fiber | 349mg sodium

Chicken Salad with a Twist

What's the twist? A little bit of mango chutney mixed in with the mayo, that's what. The chutney adds just the right sweet taste to the spicy hot sauce and bright lemon juice. This chicken salad sandwich is so good that sometimes I even skip the bread and serve it wrapped up in a lettuce leaf. I mean, go on ahead and sandwich this delicious salad between two slices if you're craving some carbs, but I highly suggest you give it a whirl scooped into some Boston lettuce leaves. The crunchy lettuce leaf is a perfect complement to this rich, flavorful chicken salad. **Serves 4**

In a large bowl, stir together the chicken, mayonnaise, celery, chutney, red onions, parsley, lemon juice, salt, and hot sauce. Serve sandwiched between bread slices or spooned into Boston lettuce leaves.

2 cups finely chopped cooked boneless, skinless chicken breast

⅓ cup light mayonnaise

¼ cup finely chopped celery

¼ cup mango chutney

2 tablespoons finely chopped red onions

2 tablespoons finely chopped fresh parsley

¾ teaspoon fresh lemon juice

¼ teaspoon salt

5 dashes of hot sauce

8 slices low-calorie whole-wheat bread or 8 large Boston lettuce leaves

BREAKIN' IT DOWN

Using Bread

	Before	After
Fat	31g	12g
Calories	483	282

26g protein | 29g carbohydrate
2g fiber | 498mg sodium

Using Lettuce

	Before	After
Fat	31g	6g
Calories	483	196

23g protein | 11g carbohydrate
0g fiber | 350mg sodium

Love My Leftovers

This chicken salad is a perfect place to use my leftover Sunday Roast Chicken (page 55). Since I always roast more chicken than I could possibly eat in one sitting, it's the meal that keeps on giving throughout the whole week.

Hummus Veggie Wrap

Now I have to admit, I didn't come across chickpeas too often when I was growing up in Albany, Georgia. But when I did discover them, I absolutely fell for their rich, nutty flavor. Then I found out they were packed full of fiber, protein, and zinc as well as being low in fat. By whipping them up into a hummus spread, you can enjoy them on all sorts of things. But this veggie wrap has got to be one of my favorite ways to savor this versatile bean. **Serves 6**

1 garlic clove, coarsely chopped

1 can (15 ounces) chickpeas, rinsed and drained

1 to 2 tablespoons fresh lemon juice, plus more as needed

3 tablespoons sesame tahini

2 tablespoons plain low-fat Greek yogurt

2 tablespoons olive oil

½ teaspoon paprika

Salt, as needed

6 (8-inch) low-carb tortillas

1½ cups coarsely chopped romaine lettuce leaves

¾ cup coarsely chopped red bell peppers

¾ cup coarsely chopped peeled cucumbers

1. In the bowl of a food processor, combine the garlic, chickpeas, lemon juice, tahini, and yogurt. Pulse until the chickpeas are coarsely chopped. Add the oil in a thin stream and process until smooth. Season with the paprika and salt. Taste and adjust the seasonings.

2. Lay a tortilla on a work surface in front of you. Slather with 3 tablespoons of the hummus. Top with ¼ cup of the lettuce, 2 tablespoons of the bell peppers, and 2 tablespoons of the cucumbers. Fold the bottom of the tortilla up over the filling. Fold in the sides, then roll up. Repeat with the remaining tortillas, hummus, and vegetables.

BREAKIN' IT DOWN

	Before	After
Fat	25g	12g
Calories	524	266

10g protein | 32g carbohydrate
17g fiber | 546mg sodium

Nutritional count does not include salt as needed.

Wrap It Quick

If you're short on time, go ahead and use store-bought hummus instead of making your own. That way you'll be able to get a nutritious and tasty lunch on the table even faster.

CHAPTER 7

Serve Up the Sides

WHILE I WOULD PROBABLY NEVER be satisfied with a solitary plate of veggies as my meal, I would also never consider a meal complete without veggies. In fact, I sometimes get a craving for a particular side dish and I use that as the starting point for my meal by grilling up a piece of fish or chicken and laying it right on top of my warm veggies, turning my side dish into a meal.

If there is one side that I could easily accept as my main meal, it would have to be French fries. I have to admit that they are my weakness. During the week, I satisfy that weakness by making my **Oven Cheese Fries** (page 131). Because they are roasted, they aren't greasy, making for a lighter, healthier alternative to fries that still tastes out of this world. Mostly, though, I turn to sweet potatoes and yams for my potato fix because they make me feel full longer. That's important when you have an active lifestyle like mine. **Baked Sweet Potato Fries** (page 132) are at the top of my snack list.

In the South, we love our dark green vegetables like collards, kale, spinach, and broccoli. And that's a good thing, too. Turns out these are just about the best vegetables for you. Loaded with iron, calcium, folate, fiber, and vitamins A and C, these leafy greens are a powerhouse for the body. It doesn't get any more Southern than my **Big Ol' Pot of Greens** (page 127). But while the traditional Southern cook might have these going on the stove from morning till night, I've streamlined the process for the busy workweek. After only twenty minutes, these greens are silky, smoky, and spicy and so, so good for you.

Of course, I couldn't leave out beans and rice in the chapter on sides. They are a mainstay of the Southern diet and they still feature prominently in mine. Thank goodness I found a way to lighten up hoppin' John. Old Southern tradition tells us to eat a bowl of this tasty bean dish on New Year's Day to ensure good luck throughout the year. Hopefully, my healthy **Hoppin' John** (page 141) will bring you good luck *and* good health. You'll be surprised by how rich and decadent tasting lightened-up **Dirty Rice** (page 144) is. If you haven't had the pleasure of savoring this Southern specialty before, you're not going to want to miss this one.

And what meal would be complete without some **Real Southern Corn Bread** (page 134)? Without corn bread, there's no way to sop up the delicious gravies and sauces on the plate. We Southerners don't like to let a scrap of food go to waste, and corn bread certainly helps us out in that regard.

Creamed Spinach

When I allow myself a splurge and I hit a steak house with the guys, creamed spinach is an absolute must-order. There is just nothing like a big, juicy rib-eye steak served with a heaping helping of creamed spinach. Well, now I can have my creamed spinach at home and feel good about it. I was able to find a way to make this side dish lighter and healthier with fat-free Greek yogurt, giving me the room in my diet to indulge in that tasty steak sitting right beside it. **Serves 4**

2 teaspoons olive oil

1 cup finely chopped onions

2 garlic cloves, finely chopped

2 packages (10 ounces each) frozen spinach, thawed, drained, and squeezed dry

Freshly ground black pepper to taste

6 tablespoons fat-free Greek yogurt (or use low-fat; optional)

2 tablespoons fat-free cream cheese (or use low-fat; optional)

½ teaspoon fresh lemon juice

1. In a medium nonstick skillet, heat the oil over medium heat. Add the onions and cook, stirring occasionally, until softened, 3 to 5 minutes. Add the garlic and cook for 30 seconds more. Add the spinach and pepper to taste and stir until the spinach is heated through.

2. Turn the heat to medium-low and add the yogurt, cream cheese, and lemon juice. Stir until the cream cheese is melted and the spinach is warmed through.

BREAKIN' IT DOWN

	Before	After
Fat	15g	2.5g
Calories	185	93

7g protein | 10g carbohydrate
2g fiber | 350mg sodium

Give It a Squeeze

Make sure you get as much water as you can out of the spinach before you add it to the skillet. Place it in a colander and give it several good squeezes with your hands, just like you're wringing out the laundry.

Broccoli Soufflé

Now I know that soufflés have a reputation for being temperamental and tricky to pull off, but the truth is, this soufflé couldn't be easier. Just whip up your egg whites to form soft peaks and fold them gently through the batter so that they don't deflate, and your soufflé will be a light and airy thing of beauty. The slightly sour, tangy taste of the goat cheese pairs so nicely with the bright lemon rind and the earthy broccoli.

Serves 6

1. Preheat the oven to 400°F and position a rack in the lower third of the oven. Lightly spray a 2½-quart soufflé dish or deep casserole with cooking spray.

2. In a medium saucepan, melt the butter over medium heat. Whisk in the flour and cook, stirring, for 1 minute. Whisk in the milk, bring to a boil, and cook, stirring constantly with the whisk, until thickened, about 2 minutes. Stir in the lemon zest, oregano, and pepper to taste.

3. Pour the hot mixture into a large bowl and beat in the egg yolks, one at a time, whisking constantly so that they don't cook. Whisk until they are completely incorporated, then whisk in the goat cheese and broccoli.

4. In the bowl of an electric mixer fitted with the whisk attachment, beat the 6 egg whites on high speed until frothy. Add a pinch of salt and continue beating until soft peaks form.

5. Using a rubber spatula, gently fold one-third of the beaten egg whites into the broccoli mixture until incorporated. Gently fold in the remaining egg whites. Pour into the prepared dish and bake for 30 minutes, or until puffed and golden.

2 tablespoons unsalted butter

3 tablespoons all-purpose flour

1 cup 1% milk

½ teaspoon grated lemon zest

¼ teaspoon dried oregano

Freshly ground black pepper to taste

4 large eggs, separated

4 ounces goat cheese, crumbled

1 cup cooked broccoli florets, coarsely chopped

2 large egg whites

Quick Whisk

To make quick work of beating egg whites to soft peaks, bring your eggs to room temperature before beating. Also, make sure the bowl you are beating them in is perfectly clean. Lastly, don't skip the pinch of salt. It will help speed you on your way.

BREAKIN' IT DOWN

	Before	After
Fat	19g	11g
Calories	467	177

10g protein | 7g carbohydrate
1g fiber | 160mg sodium

Mediterranean Grilled Veggies

Sweet, smoky, tender vegetables can be created only on the grill. This colorful medley of vegetables is the perfect accompaniment to a fine piece of grilled meat. It is also great to have in the fridge to add to sandwiches and salads throughout the week. **Serves 4**

1 tablespoon red wine vinegar

½ teaspoon dried oregano

½ teaspoon dried basil

⅛ teaspoon crushed red pepper flakes

3 tablespoons olive oil

1 medium yellow summer squash, thinly sliced lengthwise

1 medium zucchini, thinly sliced lengthwise

1 small eggplant, thinly sliced lengthwise

¾ teaspoon salt

¼ cup crumbled fat-free feta cheese (or use low-fat; optional)

1. In a small bowl, whisk together the vinegar, oregano, basil, and red pepper flakes. Whisk in the oil. Arrange the sliced squash, zucchini, and eggplant in a single layer on a rimmed baking sheet. Brush both sides of the vegetables lightly with the marinade. Cover and let stand for 20 minutes.

2. Spray the grill grate with cooking spray and preheat the grill to medium-high heat. Sprinkle the vegetables with the salt. Place on the grill and cook, covered, until lightly charred and tender, 2 to 3 minutes per side. Place on a serving platter, sprinkle with the feta, and serve.

BREAKIN' IT DOWN

	Before	After
Fat	16g	10g
Calories	203	150

6g protein | 11g carbohydrate
5g fiber | 579mg sodium

In the Basket

The easiest way to grill vegetables is using a grill basket. That way you can get the vegetables right onto the grate (where they'll get nicely charred) without worrying about them slipping through into the fire.

Golden Crunchy Okra

Now don't go flipping past this recipe because the okra isn't fried. I reckon this baked version is just as tasty. The high heat creates a crispy cornmeal crust while keeping the okra tender inside. When I feel like a snack, I turn to these crunchy treats to satisfy my craving. And satisfy they do. **Serves 4**

⅔ cup 1% buttermilk
⅔ cup fine cornmeal
½ teaspoon salt
⅛ teaspoon cayenne pepper
½ pound okra, trimmed

1. Preheat the oven to 400°F. Spray a rimmed baking sheet generously with cooking spray.

2. Place the buttermilk in a shallow bowl. In a separate bowl, whisk together the cornmeal, salt, and cayenne.

3. Dip the okra first in the buttermilk, then in the cornmeal mixture. Place the okra on the prepared baking sheet. Spray the tops and sides of the okra with cooking spray. Bake until golden, 10 to 15 minutes.

BREAKIN' IT DOWN

	Before	After
Fat	5g	.5g
Calories	209	73

3g protein | 14g carbohydrate
3g fiber | 446mg sodium

Buttermilk Bath

Soaking okra in buttermilk is an old Southern technique for reducing the natural sliminess of this vegetable. If you have a little more time on your hands, go ahead and soak the okra for as long as 30 minutes. The lactic acid in the buttermilk will do its job on the okra to even further reduce the chances of that slimy texture coming out.

Big Ol' Pot of Greens

I don't think there is a side dish that says Southern cooking quite like a big ol' pot of greens. And collards are my greens of choice. Some Southern cooks swear you need to cook your collards all day long to get them to just the ideal silky texture. But I think twenty minutes is just about right. More important are the smoked turkey neck or wings and the hot sauce. All that fine smoky flavor topped off with a spicy hit of hot sauce is really what makes this dish sing. **Serves 6**

1. In a large pot, melt the butter over medium heat. Add the onions and cook, stirring, until almost soft, about 5 minutes. Add the turkey and the chicken broth and simmer gently for 20 minutes.

2. Stir in the greens and cook until tender, 15 to 20 minutes. Season with the salt and hot sauce and serve.

1 tablespoon unsalted butter

1 Vidalia or other sweet onion, halved and thinly sliced

½ pound smoked turkey neck or wings

2½ cups low-sodium chicken broth

2 pounds collard greens, stems removed and leaves cut into ½-inch strips

½ teaspoon salt

Hot sauce to taste

Georgia Sweets

Vidalias are a source of great pride to native Georgia folk. But I realize that you may not be able to get them where you live. If that's the case, some other onions that will do in a pinch include Super Sweets from Texas, Maui sweets from Hawaii, or Walla Walla sweets from Washington State.

BREAKIN' IT DOWN

	Before	After
Fat	34g	5g
Calories	471	149

14g protein | 12g carbohydrate
6g fiber | 296mg sodium

Nutritional count does not include hot sauce to taste.

SERVE UP THE SIDES

127

Almost-Famous Tomato Pie

The original famous tomato pie belongs, of course, to my Mama. But I think this tomato pie right here might just be knocking on fame's door. I like to bring this pie to picnics and barbecues because it's best eaten outside at room temperature on a beautiful day. **Serves 8**

1 (9-inch) whole-wheat pie shell

1 teaspoon cornstarch

1 cup fat-free Greek yogurt (or use low-fat; optional)

¼ cup light mayonnaise

2 cups crumbled feta cheese

⅓ cup finely chopped scallions (white and light green parts only)

4 medium tomatoes, seeded and thickly sliced

¾ teaspoon The Lady's House Seasoning (page 16)

⅓ cup loosely packed fresh basil, coarsely chopped

1. Preheat the oven to 350°F.

2. Bake the pie shell for 10 minutes.

3. Meanwhile, in a medium bowl, sprinkle the cornstarch over the yogurt and stir until thoroughly combined. Stir in the mayonnaise, feta, and scallions.

4. In the baked pie shell, layer the tomatoes, House Seasoning, and basil. Spoon the feta mixture over the top, using the back of the spoon to spread it evenly.

5. Bake for 45 minutes, or until golden brown along the edges of the topping. Let stand on a wire rack for 10 minutes before serving.

BREAKIN' IT DOWN

	Before	After
Fat	31g	16g
Calories	428	261

11g protein | 19g carbohydrate
2g fiber | 726mg sodium

Subs 'n Swaps

I love this pie with feta cheese, but it really lends itself to any old cheese you have a hankering for. Try swapping out the feta and basil for part-skim mozzarella and oregano or, for a Tex-Mex flavor, add in low-fat Monterey Jack and cilantro.

Buttermilk Mashed Potatoes

These mashed potatoes are so full of flavor, you'll actually forget there's no butter in them. That's because of my secret ingredient: low-fat garlic and herb cheese. The cheese brings so much rich, creamy flavor that I realized I didn't even need the butter, making my job of lightening up this recipe that much easier. **Serves 4**

1. In a large pot, cover the potatoes with cold salted water. Bring to a boil over medium-high heat and cook until the potatoes are tender, about 20 minutes. Drain well and return the potatoes to the pot.

2. Meanwhile, in a small saucepan, gently warm the buttermilk (make sure you don't let it get too hot or it will separate).

3. Using a potato masher, mash the warmed buttermilk and the cheese into the potatoes until you reach the consistency you like (it's okay if you like 'em lumpy!). Season to taste with pepper.

1½ **pounds russet potatoes, peeled and cut into chunks**

¾ **cup 1% buttermilk**

½ **cup Boursin Light Garlic & Herbs cheese**

Freshly ground black pepper to taste

Smooth Operator

If you're after a smoother style of mash, I recommend getting yourself a ricer or food mill. They're great little appliances that make it easy to create smooth restaurant-style mashed potatoes right in your own kitchen.

BREAKIN' IT DOWN

	Before	After
Fat	18g	5g
Calories	330	217

7g protein | 39g carbohydrate
3g fiber | 115mg sodium

Twice-Baked Cheddar Potatoes

I'll wager that your mama used to make you a version of these potatoes when you were young. And I'll bet it was chock-full of sour cream and butter! I've got fond memories of that, for sure. Well, here it is again, my good friend Greek yogurt coming to the rescue so that I can enjoy a childhood favorite. While my Mama would sprinkle the grated Cheddar on top of the potato, I stir it into the potato mixture so that I can replace some of the fat I've taken out by removing the butter and sour cream. These potatoes are hearty and warming, perfect on a cold winter day. **Serves 4**

4 medium russet potatoes

1 cup grated low-fat Cheddar cheese

½ cup fat-free Greek yogurt (or use low-fat; optional)

⅓ cup skim milk

¾ teaspoon salt

Freshly ground black pepper to taste

Paprika to taste

3 scallions (white and light green parts only), thinly sliced, for serving

1. Preheat the oven to 350°F.

2. Cut a slit in the top of each potato and lightly spray the skin all over with cooking spray. Arrange the potatoes on an ungreased rimmed baking sheet and bake until tender, about 1 hour.

3. Slice off the top third of each potato. Scoop out the insides into a medium bowl and mash with the Cheddar, yogurt, milk, salt, and pepper. Return the potato shells to the baking sheet. Scrape the mixture back into the potato shells. Sprinkle with paprika and bake until golden, 20 to 30 minutes. Top with the scallions and serve.

BREAKIN' IT DOWN

	Before	After
Fat	11g	1g
Calories	287	209

12g protein | 39g carbohydrate
4g fiber | 1024mg sodium

Make It a Meal

Just as Mama used to do, I add whatever leftovers I have in the fridge to my stuffed potatoes to make this a meal. Choose from chopped broccoli or mushrooms to ground turkey or chopped shrimp to just about anything in between.

Oven Cheese Fries

These out-of-this-world cheese fries are prepared with only a light coating of cooking spray. You can get away with so little oil because the potatoes are tossed in a spicy cheese mixture in a resealable plastic bag. This helps to ensure that they get a good coating to stick to them all over. Every bite of these delicious fries packs a wallop of flavor. **Serves 4**

1. Preheat the oven to 375°F.

2. Place the Parmesan, paprika, thyme, salt, and pepper in a large resealable plastic bag and shake the bag to combine the mixture.

3. Arrange the potatoes in a single layer on a rimmed baking sheet. Spray lightly on all sides with cooking spray. Working in batches, add several wedges to the plastic bag and shake well until they are coated with the cheese mixture.

4. Return the wedges to the baking sheet and bake, turning once halfway through, until golden and tender, 40 to 50 minutes.

5 tablespoons grated Parmesan cheese

1 teaspoon paprika

1 teaspoon dried thyme

½ teaspoon salt

½ teaspoon freshly ground black pepper

2 russet potatoes, each cut into 8 wedges

Keep the Favorites

Because French fries are a favorite food of mine, I had to find a way to keep them in my diet. It's important that you do that for your favorite food, too, whether it is chocolate, bacon, or beef. If your diet starts to feel like one big lesson in deprivation, you will be setting yourself up for failure. Find ways to prepare your favorite foods in a healthier way and enjoy them in moderation.

BREAKIN' IT DOWN

	Before	After
Fat	22g	2g
Calories	352	107

5g protein | 19g carbohydrate
2g fiber | 626mg sodium

SERVE UP THE SIDES

Baked Sweet Potato Fries

Sweet, salty, and spicy, these sweet potato fries are just brimming with flavor. By baking them at a high temperature, they crisp up nicely on the outside but stay creamy on the inside, just as they would if you fried them, but without all the greasiness. I reckon these fries are a perfect guilt-free snack. **Serves 4**

2 large sweet potatoes,
  peeled

1 tablespoon olive oil

¾ teaspoon salt

⅛ teaspoon cayenne pepper

Pinch of ground cinnamon

1. Preheat the oven to 425°F.

2. Slice the potatoes into ¾-inch-wide slices and toss with the oil, salt, cayenne, and cinnamon. Spread on a large ungreased rimmed baking sheet.

3. Roast, tossing occasionally, until tender and golden, about 25 minutes.

BREAKIN' IT DOWN

	Before	After
Fat	**23g**	**3g**
Calories	**445**	**105**

4g protein | 16g carbohydrate
2g fiber | 467mg sodium

Spice of Life

You can change up these fries in so many ways by experimenting with different spices. Switch out the cinnamon for nutmeg or a smoky paprika. Or try Cajun seasoning for a kick of the Bayou. At a party, I like to serve these with a spicy yogurt dip.

Real Southern Corn Bread

We Southerners would be at a complete loss without corn bread. I mean, how would we sop up all the delicious gravies and sauces we love so much in our dishes? Corn bread is key. So, of course, I just had to find a way to lighten it up. And here it is.
Serves 8

1 cup all-purpose flour

⅔ cup fine cornmeal

½ teaspoon baking soda

½ teaspoon salt

¼ teaspoon freshly ground black pepper

¾ cup 1% milk

1 large egg, lightly beaten

1 tablespoon honey

1. Preheat the oven to 425°F. Spray an 8-inch square baking pan with cooking spray.

2. In a medium bowl, whisk together the flour, cornmeal, baking soda, salt, and pepper. In a large bowl, whisk together the milk, egg, and honey, then whisk the flour mixture into the milk mixture.

3. Scrape the batter into the prepared pan. Bake for 20 to 25 minutes, until a toothpick inserted into the center of the bread comes out clean. Let cool for 10 minutes before serving.

BREAKIN' IT DOWN

	Before	After
Fat	7g	1g
Calories	182	112

4g protein | 21g carbohydrate
1g fiber | 247mg sodium

Subs 'n Swaps

For an even healthier version of this corn bread, substitute half of the all-purpose flour with whole-wheat flour. Using a mix of both flours is healthier, and will still result in the nice light texture that you get from using all-purpose flour.

Corn Bread Dressing

Roast turkey? I like it just fine. But my absolute favorite part of the Thanksgiving meal is the dressing. And corn bread dressing tops that list. This quick version of the holiday classic lets me enjoy dressing any day of the year I like. **Serves 10**

1. Preheat the oven to 400°F. Spray a 9-inch square baking pan with cooking spray.

2. Spread the corn bread cubes on a rimmed baking sheet and toast until golden, about 10 minutes.

3. In a large skillet, brown the sausage over medium-high heat, for about 5 minutes, breaking up the sausage with a fork. Stir in the butter until melted, then add the onions and celery and cook until the vegetables are softened, 5 to 7 minutes. Stir in the garlic and sage and cook for 1 minute more.

4. In a large bowl, stir together the toasted corn bread, the sausage mixture, the chicken broth, egg, egg white, salt, and pepper until combined. Spoon the dressing into the prepared pan and bake for 25 to 30 minutes, until golden and firm.

1 batch Real Southern Corn Bread (page 134), cut into ¾-inch cubes

6 ounces Italian turkey sausage (about 2 links), casings removed

1 tablespoon unsalted butter

2 cups finely chopped onions

⅔ cup finely chopped celery

1 garlic clove, finely chopped

1 tablespoon finely chopped fresh sage

½ cup low-sodium chicken broth

1 large egg

1 large egg white

¾ teaspoon salt

½ teaspoon freshly ground black pepper

Case Closed

To extract the sausage meat from its casing, hold the sausage over a bowl and give the sausage a good squeeze from one end. The meat will pop out of the other end, leaving the empty casing in your hand.

BREAKIN' IT DOWN

	Before	After
Fat	19g	3.5g
Calories	342	114

6g protein | 15g carbohydrate
1g fiber | 502mg sodium

SERVE UP THE SIDES

Corn Casserole

This corn casserole is my version of classic Southern spoon bread. It's chewy on the edges, creamy in the center, and jumping with sweet corn flavor. In fact, the only thing missing from this recipe is two-thirds of the fat you usually find. **Serves 6 to 8**

1 cup low-fat sour cream

¼ cup unsweetened applesauce

1 large egg, lightly beaten

1 box (8½ ounces) "Jiffy" corn muffin mix

1 can (15¼ ounces) corn kernels

1 can (14¾ ounces) creamed corn

1. Preheat the oven to 350°F. Lightly spray a 9-inch square baking pan with cooking spray.

2. In a medium bowl, whisk together the sour cream, applesauce, and egg until combined. Add the muffin mix, corn kernels, and creamed corn and stir gently to combine.

3. Pour the mixture into the prepared pan. Bake for about 60 minutes, until golden and a toothpick inserted into the center comes out clean. Let cool for 5 minutes before serving.

BREAKIN' IT DOWN

	Before	After
Fat	19g	9g
Calories	323	282

6g protein | 47g carbohydrate
1.5g fiber | 660mg sodium

Nutritional count based on 7 servings

Creamy Southern Squash and Onions

I usually pair this side dish with a simple piece of roasted meat. But I absolutely always serve it with corn bread. The creamy sauce is the real star of the show here, and I find I need a good hunk of corn bread to sop it all up. **Serves 4**

In a large skillet, heat the butter over medium-high heat. Add the onions and a pinch of salt and cook until golden, about 5 minutes. Stir in the garlic and squash and cook until the squash is tender, but not too soft. Stir in the evaporated milk, Monterey Jack, ¼ teaspoon salt, and lots of pepper. Cook until the mixture is bubbling and slightly thick, about 3 minutes.

1 tablespoon unsalted butter

2 cups finely chopped onions

¼ teaspoon salt, plus a pinch

1 garlic clove, finely chopped

2 pounds yellow summer squash, cut into ½-inch chunks

½ cup fat-free evaporated milk (or use low-fat; optional)

½ cup grated low-fat Monterey Jack cheese

Freshly ground black pepper to taste

Summer Lovin'

There are so many types of squash out there that I know it can get confusing. Be sure to look for the immature yellow squash, sometimes known as summer squash, for this recipe. The mature autumn and winter squash have thick, inedible rinds that won't work here. If you can't get your hands on yellow squash, this recipe also tastes great with pattypan squash or zucchini.

BREAKIN' IT DOWN

	Before	After
Fat	**31g**	**7g**
Calories	**438**	**168**

8g protein | 18g carbohydrate
3g fiber | 315mg sodium

Succotash

In the South, we like to call any vegetable mixture with lima beans a succotash. But I make sure mine always has sweet corn as well. And if I can find it, I choose shoe-peg corn, a Southern favorite, known for its smaller kernels and unmatched sweetness. If you can't find frozen shoepeg, that's just fine. This recipe stands up on its own with any variety of corn. **Serves 6**

1 box (10 ounces) frozen lima beans

1 tablespoon olive oil

2 turkey bacon slices

1 box (10 ounces) frozen corn

2 tablespoons low-sodium chicken broth

1 teaspoon The Lady's House Seasoning (page 16)

1 medium tomato, coarsely chopped

1. In a large pot of boiling salted water, cook the lima beans until tender, about 8 minutes.

2. Meanwhile, in a large skillet, heat the oil over medium heat. Add the bacon and cook, turning, until brown, about 5 minutes. Drain on a paper towel–lined plate, then coarsely chop. Set aside the skillet with the drippings.

3. When the limas are tender, drain and add to the skillet, along with the corn, chicken broth, and House Seasoning. Cook over medium heat, stirring, for 2 minutes. Add the tomato and chopped bacon and cook, stirring, until heated through, another 2 to 3 minutes.

BREAKIN' IT DOWN

	Before	After
Fat	34g	4g
Calories	477	130

6g protein | 20g carbohydrate
4g fiber | 359mg sodium

First Things First

Here's my trick for getting myself to eat more vegetables. Every time I sit down to a meal, I eat my veggies first. That way, if I start to fill up, I fill up on vegetables, rather than the higher-calorie foods on my plate.

Green Bean and Onion Casserole

This updated version of the green bean casserole is so awesomely rich and cheesy, you'll think of it as an indulgence. While you tend to see this casserole on the table at Thanksgiving, I like to serve it on any given day paired with my Sunday Roast Chicken (page 55). After all, one day a year is just not enough for giving thanks. **Serves 4 to 6**

8 ounces white button mushrooms, quartered

1 small onion, thinly sliced

½ teaspoon The Lady's House Seasoning (page 16)

8 ounces green beans, cut into 1½- to 2-inch pieces (about 2 heaping cups)

1 can (10½ ounces) low-fat cream of mushroom soup

¼ cup 1% milk

1 teaspoon low-sodium soy sauce

1 cup grated low-fat Swiss cheese

1. Preheat the oven to 450°F. Spray two rimmed baking sheets with cooking spray.

2. Place the mushrooms on one baking sheet and the onions on the other. Spray lightly with cooking spray and season with ¼ teaspoon of the House Seasoning. Place in the oven. After 5 minutes, give the mushroom baking sheet a shake and turn the onion baking sheet around (this will help them to cook evenly). Roast until browned, about 3 minutes more for the mushrooms and 7 minutes more for the onions. Lower the oven temperature to 350°F.

3. Meanwhile, in a large pot of boiling salted water, cook the green beans until tender, 5 to 7 minutes, and drain.

4. In a medium bowl, stir together the drained green beans, the mushrooms, onions, mushroom soup, milk, soy sauce, and remaining ¼ teaspoon House Seasoning.

5. Lightly coat a baking dish with cooking spray and fill with the green bean mixture. Bake for 20 minutes, then top with the Swiss cheese and bake until melted and bubbly, about 10 minutes.

BREAKIN' IT DOWN

	Before	After
Fat	18g	3g
Calories	252	111

10g protein | 13g carbohydrate
2g fiber | 504mg sodium

Nutritional count based on 5 servings

Hoppin' John

In my mind, New Year's Day and hoppin' John go together like, well, like beans and rice. My Mama used to tell us that eating hoppin' John on New Year's Day would bring us good luck in the year to come. Since I think I've been pretty blessed in this life, I still have a bowl of this down-home classic every New Year's Day. And now that I've lightened it up, hoppin' John is a staple in my weekday diet. Now, how lucky is that? **Serves 4**

1. In a large skillet, cook the bacon over medium-low heat until crisp, about 5 minutes. Stir in the butter, onions, bell peppers, thyme, and garlic powder. Cook until the vegetables are soft, 5 to 7 minutes.

2. Stir in the black-eyed peas, rice, and chicken broth. Simmer until the mixture is hot and most of the liquid is evaporated. Season with the salt and give it a nice dash of hot sauce.

4 turkey bacon slices, coarsely chopped

1 teaspoon unsalted butter

¾ cup finely chopped onions

½ cup finely chopped green bell peppers

½ teaspoon dried thyme

⅛ teaspoon garlic powder

2 cups frozen black-eyed peas

1½ cups cooked white or brown rice

¼ cup low-sodium chicken broth or water

¼ teaspoon salt

Hot sauce to taste

Good Luck Greens

Many Southerners like to serve this dish with greens like mustard or collards. In fact, there's yet another superstition that holds that eating greens on New Year's Day, because they represent the color of money, will bring wealth throughout the new year. Personally, I like to serve greens with hoppin' John because they add vitamins and taste so darn good.

BREAKIN' IT DOWN

	Before	After
Fat	10g	5g
Calories	475	280

13g protein | 46g carbohydrate
8g fiber | 433mg sodium

Nutritional count using white rice, and not including hot sauce to taste

SERVE UP THE SIDES

141

Quick Pickled Cucumbers

I remember my Mama making us a creamy cucumber salad, and when I was little, it was my favorite kind of salad. Mama, however, did not use Greek yogurt in hers. Her creaminess came from sour cream and mayonnaise. But you know what? I served this version to my Mama recently, and she couldn't stop raving about it. She loved it so much, I reckon I might see a tub of Greek yogurt lurking around her fridge next time I'm home. **Serves 4**

2 medium cucumbers, peeled and sliced thinly

1 tablespoon white wine vinegar

1 teaspoon salt

½ cup fat-free Greek yogurt

1 tablespoon chopped fresh dill

1. In a medium bowl, toss the cucumbers with the vinegar and salt. Cover with plastic wrap and let the cucumbers stand at room temperature for 30 minutes.

2. Pour off any excess liquid and stir in the yogurt and dill. Cover with plastic wrap and refrigerate the salad until you are ready to serve.

BREAKIN' IT DOWN

	Before	After
Fat	**8g**	**0g**
Calories	**146**	**32**

3g protein | 4g carbohydrate
1g fiber | 593mg sodium

Peel Appeal

If you like the skin on your cucumber, go ahead and leave it on. After all, the skin is where the nutrients are. You'll find fiber and beta carotene in the peel and you'll give your salad a little extra crunch. If you plan to leave the peel on, it's best to use Kirby cucumbers.

Dirty Rice

Now, you might already know that what makes this rice "dirty" is the chicken livers chopped up in it. What you might not know is that the chicken livers are also what make this rice dish so darn good. Chicken livers are not only rich in flavor, but they are very inexpensive, making this is a true Southern dish: tasty, quick to prepare, and economical. **Serves 4 to 6**

1 teaspoon canola oil

6 ounces andouille chicken sausage, finely chopped

4 ounces chicken livers, finely chopped (see box below)

6 scallions, white and light green parts thinly sliced, dark greens reserved for serving

½ cup finely chopped celery

½ cup finely chopped green bell peppers

3 cups hot cooked long-grain rice

3 tablespoons coarsely chopped fresh parsley

Freshly ground black pepper or hot sauce to taste

1. In a large pot, heat the oil over medium-high heat. Add the sausage and cook until golden, 5 to 7 minutes. Stir in the chicken livers and brown quickly. Add the sliced scallions, along with the celery and bell peppers. Cook until softened, about 5 minutes.

2. Fold in the rice and parsley and season to taste with pepper or hot sauce. Thinly slice the dark green scallion tops and scatter over the rice before serving.

BREAKIN' IT DOWN

	Before	After
Fat	16g	5g
Calories	390	273

16g protein | 37g carbohydrate
2g fiber | 391mg sodium

Nutritional count based on 5 servings, with hot sauce to taste

Proper Preppin'

If you've never prepared chicken livers before, you want to make sure that you clean them properly before you cook them. It's important to remove the bitter-tasting connective tissue between the two lobes of the liver. Place the liver on a cutting board and gently spread the lobes apart. Hold one lobe steady while pressing the side of a small sharp knife against the other lobe to separate them. Gently scrape the tissue from the lobe to which the tissue is still attached. Give the lobes a rinse and pat them dry.

CHAPTER 8

Morning Glory! A Better Breakfast

THERE WAS A TIME when I just didn't see the point in eating breakfast. I guess I was so eager to get my day started I'd rush right on by it. Out the door I'd go with nothing in my body to get it going, much less keep it going. Then I'd hit the gym and work up a monster appetite. I'd be so hungry after my workouts that I didn't care what I ate after getting out of there. And that was not a good position to put my body in.

But now, I'm proud to say that I've seen the light on breakfast. I make sure that I wake up each and every morning and get myself together a hearty, healthy breakfast. And you know what? I feel so much better for it. I have loads more energy, and I find I'm not starving by the time the afternoon rolls around. Why, a satisfying breakfast even helps me make the right choices when it comes to dinner.

But we're all busy, right? Besides Sunday morning, who has time to spend hours on breakfast? So these recipes are not only healthy and satisfying, but fast and easy. They'll make you feel like it's Sunday brunch every day of the week. Take, for instance, my slimmed-down version of **Tomato Grits and Sausage** (page 152). It doesn't get more down home and comforting than that. But at 170 calories and 9 grams of fat, you won't feel weighed down after a plate of this in the morning. The same goes for my **French Toast Casserole** (page 159). My Mama does amazin' breakfast casseroles like this one. As a kid, I dreamt about these casseroles all night when I knew she was fixing to serve one the next day. I think my version stands up pretty well, and it won't have you loosening your belt buckle after you eat it.

What I really love most in the morning is a good farm-raised egg. Sometimes I whip up my **Easy Eggs Florentine** (page 156) or my **Toasted-Waffle Ham and Egg Sandwich** (page 158). They make me feel like I just had a big old diner breakfast, except I've taken in fewer than half the calories. Other times, I simply boil an egg, sprinkle it with a little salt and pepper, and eat it walking out the door. Pure protein. Pure delicious.

The fact is, breakfast truly is the most important meal of the day. It's the fuel you need to make the most of your day. So, I say, why not make it delicious, too?

Maple Ham Biscuits

These biscuits smell so darn good when they're baking that they will wake up even the greatest of sleepyheads in your house. They bring together my favorite taste combination—the subtle sweetness of maple syrup and the saltiness of ham. **Makes about 12 / Serves 12**

3 cups all-purpose flour

1 tablespoon plus 1 teaspoon baking powder

1 teaspoon baking soda

¾ teaspoon salt

5 tablespoons cold unsalted butter, cut into small pieces

1½ cups 1% buttermilk

2 teaspoons light maple syrup

½ cup finely chopped ham

1. Preheat the oven to 425°F. Lightly spray a rimmed baking sheet with cooking spray.

2. In a large bowl, whisk together the flour, baking powder, baking soda, and salt. Cut in the butter with a fork until the mixture resembles coarse meal. Stir in the buttermilk and maple syrup until just combined. Fold the ham into the dough.

3. Turn the dough out onto a lightly floured surface. Knead it a few times, then roll it out to a ¾-inch thickness. Using a 2-inch round biscuit cutter, cut the dough into biscuits. Place the biscuits on the prepared baking sheet and spray the tops lightly with cooking spray. Bake for 12 to 15 minutes, until golden and firm to the touch.

BREAKIN' IT DOWN

	Before	After
Fat	15g	6g
Calories	352	180

5g protein | 26g carbohydrate
1g fiber | 480mg sodium

Shortcut

"Cutting in" is a baking term for combining butter or some other shortening with dry ingredients. Using a fork is a quick way to work in your butter, but you can also use a pastry blender, your fingertips, or a pair of knives. The most important thing to remember when cutting in is to work quickly to get the butter incorporated before it begins to melt.

Good Morning Pumpkin-Corn Muffins

These tasty muffins are moist and crumbly with a hint of spicy cinnamon to wake you up in the morning. They can be made ahead of time and reheated the day of or just eaten cold running out the door. These days, when I know I've got a busy morning ahead of me the next day, I make a batch of these satisfying muffins the night before, giving me the convenience of an instant breakfast the next day, right along with the comfort of homemade baking. **Makes 12 / Serves 12**

1. Preheat the oven to 350°F. Spray a 12-cup muffin pan with cooking spray.

2. In a medium bowl, whisk together the flour, cornmeal, sugar, baking powder, baking soda, cinnamon, and salt. In another medium bowl, combine the pumpkin, buttermilk, oil, eggs, vanilla, and orange zest. Using a rubber spatula, fold the pumpkin mixture into the flour mixture until just combined.

3. Spoon the batter into the prepared muffin pan, dividing evenly, and bake for about 20 minutes, until a toothpick inserted into the center of a muffin comes out clean. Let the muffins cool in the pan for 5 minutes, then turn the pan over to pop them out onto a wire rack to cool for another 10 minutes. Muffins can be stored (once completely cooled) in an airtight container for several days.

1½ cups all-purpose flour

½ cup cornmeal

½ cup sugar

1½ teaspoons baking powder

½ teaspoon baking soda

½ teaspoon ground cinnamon

¼ teaspoon salt

¾ cup canned pumpkin

½ cup 1% buttermilk

¼ cup vegetable oil

2 large eggs, lightly beaten

1 teaspoon pure vanilla extract

Grated zest of 1 orange

Spread the Word

My Mama used to serve me my breakfast muffin all warm and toasty, with a generous spread of butter melting all over it. These days, I make a lighter spread by mixing low-fat ricotta, honey, and a squeeze of fresh orange juice—a perfect addition to any muffin.

BREAKIN' IT DOWN

	Before	After
Fat	8g	6g
Calories	218	161

3g protein | 24g carbohydrate
1g fiber | 221mg sodium

Bobby's Morning Ritual Smoothie

Here's a recipe for a protein-packed morning smoothie that I love to make up and take with me out the door. It's a sweet, creamy concoction that I never tire of. With the addition of the whey protein powder, it's a complete breakfast in a glass.
Serves 4

1 cup fresh orange juice or juice of your choice

1 cup fresh or frozen blueberries

1 cup coarsely chopped cantaloupe

1 medium banana, thickly sliced

1 cup quartered strawberries

1 cup pitted and sliced skin-on peaches

¼ cup (4 scoops) vanilla-flavored whey protein powder

Ice, for blending

Honey or agave syrup (optional)

Place the orange juice, blueberries, cantaloupe, banana, strawberries, peaches, and protein powder in a blender and top with ice. Pulse until smooth. Add honey, if you like, and pulse twice. Serve cold.

BREAKIN' IT DOWN

	Before	After
Fat	11g	3g
Calories	395	200

18g protein | 32g carbohydrate
15g fiber | 82mg sodium

Nutritional count does not include honey or agave syrup

Warm-You-Up Cinnamon Streusel Oatmeal

I'm not ashamed to admit that on some particularly busy mornings I turn to a trusty packet of oatmeal for my first meal of the day. Now, that's all fine and does the trick of getting me some energy to start the day. But nothing beats a piping-hot bowl of homemade oatmeal. If truth be told, it doesn't take all that much longer to whip up these individual-sized, streusel-topped oatmeal bowls. As an added bonus, the oatmeal is great heated in the microwave for an easy, hot breakfast throughout the week. You can store them covered in the fridge for 2 to 3 days. **Serves 4**

1. To make the streusel: In a small bowl, stir together the brown sugar, flour, and ⅛ teaspoon of the cinnamon. Add the butter substitute and stir until the mixture comes together. Stir in the pecans. The consistency of the streusel should be pasty, not crumbly. Refrigerate until ready to use.

2. To make the oatmeal: Preheat the broiler. In a medium saucepan, bring the milk, orange juice, the remaining ⅛ teaspoon cinnamon, the salt, and ¾ cup water to a boil, stirring occasionally. Stir in the oats and cook over medium heat, stirring frequently, until most of the liquid has been absorbed, 5 to 6 minutes.

3. Divide the oatmeal among four 6-ounce ramekins and top each ramekin with the streusel mixture. Broil, 6 inches from the heating element, until the topping is bubbly, 3 to 4 minutes.

Streusel

¼ **cup packed light brown sugar**

3 **tablespoons all-purpose flour**

¼ **teaspoon ground cinnamon**

2 **tablespoons low-calorie butter substitute spread**

¼ **cup pecans, coarsely chopped**

Oatmeal

1 **cup skim milk**

½ **cup fresh orange juice**

¼ **teaspoon salt**

1¼ **cups rolled oats**

Walk It Off

On your next commute into work, if you take public transportation, get off a stop early and walk the rest of the way. It's just another way to sneak a little more exercise into your day.

BREAKIN' IT DOWN

	Before	After
Fat	12g	12g
Calories	382	280

7g protein | 38g carbohydrate
4g fiber | 228mg sodium

Tomato Grits and Sausage

I've lightened up this Southern classic and given it a savory depth by swapping out cream or whole milk for chicken broth. I've also swapped out the traditional higher-calorie pork sausage and replaced it with flavor-packed turkey kielbasa. This is a stick-to-your-ribs type of breakfast that powers me up for the busiest of days. But don't feel like you have to limit this dish to the morning. It's great at any time of the day. **Serves 6**

3½ cups low-sodium chicken broth

1 can (10 ounces) Ro-Tel or other diced tomatoes with chiles

1 cup quick-cooking grits

¾ cup grated low-fat Cheddar cheese

8 ounces turkey kielbasa, coarsely chopped

½ cup coarsely chopped scallions (white and light green parts only), for serving

1. In a medium saucepan, bring the chicken broth and tomatoes to a boil over medium-high heat. Slowly whisk in the grits, reduce the heat to medium-low, and cook, stirring, until thickened, 6 to 8 minutes. Stir in the Cheddar and remove from the heat.

2. Meanwhile, in a medium nonstick skillet, cook the sausage over medium heat, stirring until browned all over, 5 to 7 minutes. Stir half of the sausage into the grits.

3. Spoon the grits into bowls and top with the remaining half of the sausage and the scallions.

BREAKIN' IT DOWN

	Before	After
Fat	52g	9g
Calories	726	170

13g protein | 10g carbohydrate
2g fiber | 756mg sodium

Make It Quick

For Southerners, quick-cooking grits are heaven sent. Most of us simply don't have the time for the long-cooking stone-ground kind. And instant tastes nothing like the real thing. Done in less than ten minutes, quick-cooking grits are a pantry staple.

Fried Salmon Cakes and Eggs

This breakfast packs a real punch because it's loaded with nutrients and protein and tastes great. To save on time in the morning, I make up my salmon patties the night before and keep them covered in the fridge so they are all ready to be browned the next morning. They are also great for lunch, served with a side salad. **Serves 4**

1 can (8 ounces) water-packed salmon, drained

3 tablespoons light mayonnaise

3 tablespoons plus ⅓ cup dried bread crumbs

1 large egg white, lightly beaten

1 tablespoon coarsely chopped fresh dill

¼ teaspoon salt

¼ teaspoon freshly ground black pepper, plus more to taste

1 tablespoon plus 1 teaspoon canola oil

4 large eggs

1. In a large bowl, combine the salmon, mayonnaise, 3 tablespoons of the bread crumbs, the egg white, dill, salt, and pepper. Form the mixture into 4 equal-size cakes. Put the remaining ⅓ cup bread crumbs in a bowl and turn the cakes in the bowl to coat each one.

2. In a large nonstick skillet, heat 1 tablespoon of the oil over medium-high heat. Add the salmon cakes and cook until golden, about 3 minutes per side. Be sure not to move them around the skillet until they set. Flip them when you can easily slide the spatula under. Place them on a plate while you make the eggs.

3. Wipe out the skillet and add the remaining 1 teaspoon oil. Crack in the eggs and season lightly with salt and pepper. Cook, uncovered, until the edges are firm. Cover and cook over low heat until set, 2 to 3 minutes. Place one egg over each salmon cake and serve.

BREAKIN' IT DOWN

	Before	After
Fat	27g	16g
Calories	389	277

21g protein | 12g carbohydrate
.5g fiber | 677mg sodium

Homemade Bread Crumbs

All you need to do to make fresh bread crumbs is pulse up some crustless bread slices in the food processor. I like to use fresh whole-wheat bread that contains no nuts or seeds. While you're at it, you might as well pulse up some extra. Place the extra bread crumbs in a resealable plastic bag in the freezer. That way the next time you need bread crumbs you'll have them on hand. They'll keep in the freezer for 6 months or so.

Western Omelet Bake

This seriously scrumptious, cheesy bake is a real treat in the morning. The bell peppers, onions, and ham load it up with great flavor. And like most breakfast bakes, this one can be prepped the night before, refrigerated, and popped into the oven in the morning, making it a great choice for breakfast and brunch entertaining. I love no-fuss dishes like this one that leave me more time to spend with my guests. **Serves 4**

1. Preheat the oven to 350°F. Lightly spray an 8-inch square baking pan with cooking spray.

2. In a medium nonstick skillet lightly coated with cooking spray, cook the bell peppers and onions over medium heat, stirring frequently, until softened, 3 to 5 minutes.

3. Meanwhile, in a medium bowl, whisk together the eggs, egg whites, milk, hot sauce, and pepper.

4. Scatter the toasted bread evenly over the bottom of the prepared baking pan. Top with the ham, followed by the bell pepper mixture, and then the Cheddar. Pour the egg mixture over the top. Bake for 1 hour, or until a knife inserted into the center comes out clean. Cut into pieces and serve.

1 cup finely chopped green bell peppers

½ cup finely chopped onions

4 large eggs

1 cup egg whites, fresh or pasteurized

1 cup 1% milk

⅛ teaspoon hot sauce

Freshly ground black pepper to taste

4 slices light whole-wheat bread, toasted and cut into 1-inch pieces

4 ounces extra-lean ham steak, finely chopped

1 cup grated low-fat Cheddar cheese

BREAKIN' IT DOWN

	Before	After
Fat	21g	10g
Calories	350	289

30g protein | 21g carbohydrate
5g fiber | 783mg sodium

Easy Eggs Florentine

The trick to slimming down this classic breakfast dish is in lightening up the hollandaise sauce. I skip the egg yolks and use low-fat milk thickened up with flour and a little pat of butter for a rich, luscious texture. Then I keep it nice and bright with a good squeeze of fresh lemon juice. **Serves 4**

1 package (10 ounces) frozen chopped spinach, thawed, drained, and squeezed dry

4 large eggs

½ teaspoon salt

¼ teaspoon freshly ground black pepper

1 tablespoon unsalted butter

1 tablespoon all-purpose flour

¾ cup 1% milk

1 tablespoon fresh lemon juice

2 multigrain English muffins, split and toasted

2 tablespoons coarsely chopped fresh basil (optional)

1. In a large nonstick skillet, heat the spinach over medium heat until warm. Using the back of a spoon, make four small indentations to create nests in the spinach. Carefully crack an egg into each nest and sprinkle ¼ teaspoon of the salt and ⅛ teaspoon of the pepper over the eggs. Cover and cook over low heat until the eggs are lightly set, about 5 minutes.

2. Meanwhile, melt the butter in a small saucepan. Whisk in the flour and cook for 1 minute. Slowly whisk in the milk. Let the mixture bubble until thickened, about 2 minutes. Take the pan off the heat and whisk in the lemon juice, the remaining ¼ teaspoon salt, and the remaining ⅛ teaspoon pepper.

3. Place one English muffin half, cut side up, on each of four plates. Top each muffin half with an egg and spinach nest. Drizzle the sauce over the eggs and sprinkle with basil, if you like. Serve immediately.

BREAKIN' IT DOWN

	Before	After
Fat	28g	10g
Calories	461	281

8g protein | 34g carbohydrate

4g fiber | 689mg sodium

Toasted-Waffle Ham and Egg Sandwich

This sandwich combines one of the South's most beloved sweet and salty flavor pairings—pancake syrup with ham and egg. I like to hit my eggs with a sprinkle of coarse sea salt at the end to really bring out their flavor. The great thing about coarse salt is that you don't need much to get a good flavor going so you won't blow your sodium intake for the day on your first meal. **Serves 4**

4 slices 98% fat-free, low-sodium smoked Virginia ham (1 ounce each)

4 large eggs

Freshly ground black pepper to taste

4 frozen toaster waffles, preferably whole grain

¼ cup light maple syrup

1. Preheat the oven to 250°F.

2. In a large nonstick skillet, cook the ham slices over medium heat until the edges curl, about 30 seconds per side. Then set in an ovenproof dish and keep warm in the oven.

3. Fry the eggs, covered, in the hot skillet over medium heat until cooked to the doneness you like. Season with pepper.

4. Meanwhile, toast the waffles according to the package directions.

5. In a small microwave-safe bowl, warm the syrup in the microwave on medium power for 15 seconds.

6. Divide the waffles among four plates, drizzle with the syrup, and top each with a slice of ham and an egg.

BREAKIN' IT DOWN

	Before	After
Fat	15g	11g
Calories	362	246

15g protein | 21g carbohydrate
1g fiber | 540mg sodium

Wakin' to Bacon

If you're a bacon fan—and really, who isn't—you can use your favorite bacon here instead of the ham. Just remember that turkey bacon is a lot lighter than pork bacon is, and I think it tastes great.

French Toast Casserole

When I was a little boy, I used to love sneaking down to the fridge at night to see what goodies I might find there for the next day. When I would discover one of my Mama's breakfast casseroles sitting in there for the morning, I would hardly be able to sleep that night. This is my version of Mama's French toast casserole, which was one of my favorites. The sweet, nutty flavor is perfect on a lazy Sunday morning. You really need to let this casserole sit for only 30 minutes or so, but if you know you're going to be short on time in the morning, feel free to pull it together the night before, just like my Mama used to do. **Serves 10**

1. Lightly spray a 9 by 13-inch baking pan with cooking spray. Arrange the bread in two long rows, slightly overlapping the slices.

2. In a large bowl, whisk together the eggs, egg whites, milk, brown sugar, pecans, vanilla, cinnamon, and salt. Pour the mixture over the bread. Cover with plastic wrap and refrigerate for at least 30 minutes.

3. Preheat the oven to 350°F.

4. Bake the casserole for 40 minutes, or until it is puffed and golden. Slice and serve. Top with warm maple syrup.

12 ounces sliced, day-old low-calorie bread

6 large eggs

2 large egg whites

3 cups skim milk

¼ cup packed light brown sugar

3 tablespoons finely chopped pecans

2 teaspoons pure vanilla extract

½ teaspoon ground cinnamon

Pinch of salt

Light maple syrup, for serving (approximately 1¼ cups)

Add Some Fruit

I never miss an opportunity to work fruit into my diet. And this dish is a perfect place to add it. Sometimes I skip the maple syrup altogether and add sweetness by topping my French toast with fresh strawberries or blueberries. Other times, I whip up a homemade berry syrup by heating the berries on the stove just until they release their juices. Then I add a dash of maple syrup and serve it warm. Check out the Pecan Waffles with Strawberry Syrup (page 160) for an example of this type of berry syrup.

BREAKIN' IT DOWN

	Before	After
Fat	42g	6g
Calories	693	236

9g protein | 37g carbohydrate
1g fiber | 325mg sodium

Nutritional count includes maple syrup for serving.

Pecan Waffles with Strawberry Syrup

When I first whipped up these little beauties, even I couldn't believe they were good for me. They taste *that* decadent. These waffles have a crunchy crust and are light and fluffy on the inside, which can be difficult to pull off with whole-wheat flour alone. But mixed with the white flour, you get a light and airy texture along with a healthier waffle. **Serves 4**

Waffles

½ cup all-purpose flour

¼ cup whole-wheat flour

¼ cup finely chopped pecans

1 tablespoon sugar

¾ teaspoon baking powder

¼ teaspoon ground cinnamon

⅛ teaspoon salt

¾ cup skim milk

1½ tablespoons canola oil

1 large egg, lightly beaten

Strawberry Syrup

1½ cups finely chopped strawberries

¼ cup light maple syrup

Large pinch of ground cinnamon

1. To make the waffles: In a medium bowl, whisk together the all-purpose flour, whole-wheat flour, pecans, sugar, baking powder, cinnamon, and salt.

2. In a small bowl, whisk together the milk, oil, and egg until combined. Using a rubber spatula, fold the milk mixture into the flour mixture until just combined.

3. Preheat a waffle iron according to the manufacturer's instructions and spray it with cooking spray. Spoon about ¼ cup batter into the hot waffle iron, spreading the batter to the edges. Cook for 3 to 4 minutes, until the steaming stops. Repeat with the remaining batter. Keep warm in a 200°F oven.

4. Meanwhile, to make the syrup: In a medium saucepan, combine the strawberries, maple syrup, and cinnamon. Cook over medium heat until the strawberries are just beginning to break down and the syrup is heated through, about 5 minutes. Serve warm over the waffles.

BREAKIN' IT DOWN

	Before	After
Fat	21g	12g
Calories	411	296

7g protein | 42g carbohydrate
3g fiber | 171mg sodium

Freeze, Please

I highly recommend doubling this recipe. That way, if you manage to have any leftovers, you can freeze the waffles in a resealable plastic freezer bag. To reheat them, place the frozen waffles straight into the toaster.

CHAPTER 9

Luscious Desserts

SO YOU'VE BEEN GOOD ALL DAY. You ate the right foods, you kept yourself active, and you maybe even lifted a weight or two. But now it's time for dessert, and keeping it healthy can be a daunting task. Well, I say go for it. You deserve it! There is no need to be deprived of a treat after a day well lived. All you need to do is have a few tools at the ready to help you dial back the indulgence.

I've always got the fixin's in the house for light and luscious desserts. When I'm pulling together these treats, I turn to fresh fruits, skim or low-fat milk, Greek yogurt, egg whites, and buttermilk. Armed with these ingredients, plus some indulgent trimmings like chocolate, nuts, sugar, and booze, I can whip up something creamy, delicious, and decadent in no time flat.

When it comes to dessert, my taste tends to lean toward the savory side of sweet. That's why I created **White Chocolate–Peppermint Popcorn Balls** (page 182). I like to make up a batch of this with my nephew Jack. Half the fun for him is in the making of this confection. The other half, in case you were wondering, is in the eating.

But while I tend to go in for something salty and sweet, my brother, Jamie, cannot get enough of his pure sweet desserts. For him, I had to include two special family indulgences. First off is a leaner version of Mama's gooey butter cake (page 164). Her cake has become almost legendary at this point, and for good reason; it trumps all other desserts for pure decadence. One of Jamie's favorite desserts is my Mama's peach cake, known here in this book as **It IS My Mama's Peach Cake** (page 180) because, as it turns out, that cake of my Mama's is actually pretty good for you. Apart from a few minor tweaks, this recipe is all Mama. There you go, Jamie, and you're welcome, big bro'.

If you're a chocoholic like so many people I know, there's not much better than **Bitter-sweet Chocolate Cheesecake** (page 170). And **Angel Food Cake with Devil Sauce** (page 172) features such a rich, creamy chocolate sauce, you'll have yourself convinced it couldn't be good for you. But it is, oh, it is.

Of course, dessert can be as simple as a bowl of fresh fruit. But dressing the fruit up as a lovely light pie makes it even more fun to eat. My **Raspberry Angel Pie** (page 166) pairs up raspberry gelatin, meringue, and fresh raspberries. It's light and airy and just bursting with real fruit flavor. I can't think of a better way to finish a barbecue or picnic.

See, folks, you don't have to take the fun out of life just because you want to eat right. With the right ingredients, you can treat yourself while being good. I guess you could say, you can have your cake and eat it, too.

Gooey Less-Butter Cake

My Mama's gooey butter cake is one of her most famous recipes. It's gooey, it's buttery, it's just exactly what it sounds like, and people line up around the block at our restaurant for a slice of this insanely good cake. Reworking this recipe was a huge risk. As it turned out, though, I think I like this version a little better. I don't have the biggest sweet tooth in the South, so I happen to like that my version has less sugar, which also helps to bring out the flavor of the cream cheese. This cake feels just as decadent as my Mama's, if a bit lighter in texture. And the filling is moist and gooey even without the stick of butter! When Mama tasted it, she couldn't believe it. **Serves 12**

Cake

1 package (18¼ ounces) yellow cake mix

½ cup 1% buttermilk

1 large egg, lightly beaten

1 tablespoon unsalted butter, melted

Filling

6 ounces low-fat cream cheese (Neufchâtel), softened

2 large eggs, lightly beaten

¾ cup confectioners' sugar

⅔ cup 1% buttermilk

1 teaspoon pure vanilla extract

2 teaspoons unsalted butter, melted

1. To make the cake: Preheat the oven to 350°F. Lightly spray a 9 by 13-inch baking dish with cooking spray.

2. Place the cake mix in a large bowl. In a small bowl, whisk together the buttermilk, egg, and butter. Add the buttermilk mixture to the cake mix, stirring just until blended. Scrape the batter into the prepared baking dish.

3. To make the filling: In the bowl of an electric mixer fitted with the paddle attachment, or using a handheld mixer, beat the cream cheese until smooth. Beat in the eggs, confectioners' sugar, buttermilk, and vanilla. Gently spread the cream cheese filling over the cake mixture.

4. Bake for 40 to 50 minutes, until the center is almost firm but still gooey. Remove from the oven, brush the top of the cake with the melted butter, and let cool for 15 minutes before serving.

BREAKIN' IT DOWN

	Before	After
Fat	15g	6g
Calories	330	254

4g protein | 46g carbohydrate
0g fiber | 422mg sodium

Sweet Sift

I've cut the confectioners' sugar in this recipe way, way down, so I like to sift a little extra on top just before serving this cake. The ladies think it looks so pretty. Just be prepared for some oohs and ahhs when you bring this one out.

Not My Mama's Banana Pudding

My Mama makes an updated version of a classic Southern banana pudding. It is rich, delicious, and (you guessed it) loaded with fat and calories. She calls her version Not Yo' Mama's Banana Pudding. Well, folks, this here is my version of banana pudding, and it certainly is not *my* Mama's pudding. This version contains a respectable 192 calories and 4 grams of fat. And I don't mind saying myself that the taste is out of this world! **Serves 10**

1. In a medium saucepan, combine the milk and ¼ cup of the sugar over medium-high heat. Bring to a simmer, but do not boil.

2. In a medium bowl, whisk together the remaining ¼ cup sugar, the cornstarch, eggs, and salt. Whisking constantly, slowly pour the hot milk mixture into the cold mixture. Return the mixture to the saucepan. Cook gently over medium-low heat, stirring constantly, until it is thick and bubbly. Again, be sure not to let the mixture come to a boil. Remove from the heat and stir in the butter and vanilla. Cool completely to room temperature, then chill, covered with plastic wrap, for 1 hour or overnight.

3. In a 9-inch square baking pan, alternate the pudding, bananas, and wafers, beginning with pudding and ending with pudding. Serve with dollops of whipped topping, if you like.

2½ cups 1% milk

½ cup sugar

2 tablespoons cornstarch

2 large eggs

¼ teaspoon salt

1 tablespoon unsalted butter

1 teaspoon pure vanilla extract

3 medium ripe bananas, sliced

35 reduced-fat Nilla wafers

¾ cup fat-free whipped topping (or use light; optional), thawed, for serving

BREAKIN' IT DOWN

	Before	After
Fat	18g	4g
Calories	385	192

4g protein | 35g carbohydrate
1g fiber | 152mg sodium

LUSCIOUS DESSERTS

Raspberry Angel Pie

I think this is a pretty smart little pie. Instead of a heavy dough-based crust, the crust here is made from lighter-than-air baked meringue. It's then filled with a bright and delicious raspberry gelatin and topped with fresh raspberries. My Mama thinks this pie is just as pretty as a picture. And I'd have to agree with her on that point. It's light, bursting with flavor, and easy on the eyes, a perfect ending to any backyard barbecue. **Serves 8**

Meringue

4 large egg whites

⅛ teaspoon cream of tartar

¾ cup sugar

Filling

1 package (3 ounces) raspberry gelatin

2 cups ice cubes

1 container (8 ounces) fat-free whipped topping (or use light; optional), thawed

Fresh raspberries, for serving (optional)

1. Preheat the oven to 275°F. Lightly spray a 9-inch pie pan with cooking spray.

2. To make the meringue: In the bowl of an electric mixer fitted with the whisk attachment, beat the egg whites until frothy. Add the cream of tartar and continue beating until soft peaks form. Beat in the sugar, 1 tablespoon at a time, continuing to beat until stiff peaks form.

3. Spoon the meringue into the prepared pie pan, using the back of a spoon or a spatula to spread the whites evenly over the bottom and up the sides of the pan. Bake for 1 hour, or until lightly colored. Turn off the oven, open the door slightly, and leave the meringue in the oven for 30 minutes to cool gradually. Remove from the oven and let cool completely on a wire rack.

4. To make the filling: Place the gelatin in a large bowl and pour ⅔ cup boiling water over the gelatin, stirring for about 2 minutes, until the gelatin is completely dissolved. Add the ice cubes and stir until the gelatin thickens, 2 to 3 minutes more. Remove any unmelted ice cubes. Whisk the whipped topping into the gelatin until it is a uniform color. Refrigerate for 10 to 20 minutes, or until the mixture is thick enough to mound into the meringue pie shell.

5. Spoon the filling into the meringue pie shell and refrigerate until set, about 2 hours. Top with fresh raspberries, if you like.

BREAKIN' IT DOWN

	Before	After
Fat	6g	0g
Calories	223	167

2g protein | 38g carbohydrate

0g fiber | 87mg sodium

Fruitful Finish

Dessert is a great time to get more fruit into your diet. So add the fresh raspberries to the top of this pie if you can. If you can't find fresh raspberries, feel free to substitute fresh strawberries, blackberries, blueberries, or any frozen berries you've got on hand.

Red Velvet Cake

I know what you're thinking, "Red velvet cake, Bobby? Really? Now, how did you make that lighter and healthier?" Well, I'll tell you. First and foremost, I cut the serving size. Usually, you see red velvet cake all layered up in what I like to call too-big-to-eat slices. By making this a single-layer cake, I've cut calories and fat fast without losing any of the luscious flavor. Then I went ahead and subbed in applesauce for the butter and trimmed down the eggs. It's about as skinny as red velvet cake gets and just as gorgeous looking, too. **Serves 8 to 10**

Cake

1¼ cups all-purpose flour

1 tablespoon unsweetened cocoa powder

½ teaspoon salt

½ teaspoon baking powder

½ teaspoon baking soda

½ cup granulated sugar

¼ cup unsweetened applesauce

1 large egg

1 large egg white

¾ cup 1% buttermilk

2 tablespoons canola oil

1 teaspoon pure vanilla extract

½ teaspoon apple cider vinegar

2 teaspoons red food coloring

Frosting

6 ounces low-fat cream cheese (Neufchâtel), softened

⅓ cup confectioners' sugar, sifted

½ teaspoon pure vanilla extract

1. To make the cake: Preheat the oven to 350°F. Lightly spray an 8-inch round cake pan with cooking spray.

2. In a large bowl, whisk together the flour, cocoa powder, salt, baking powder, and baking soda. In a separate large bowl, whisk together the granulated sugar, applesauce, egg, and egg white. Whisk in the buttermilk, oil, vanilla, and vinegar. Whisk the flour mixture into the batter, then whisk in the food coloring.

3. Scrape the batter into the prepared pan and bake for 25 to 30 minutes, until a toothpick inserted into the center comes out clean. Let the cake cool completely on a wire rack, then invert it onto a serving plate.

4. To make the frosting: In the bowl of an electric mixer fitted with the paddle attachment, or using a handheld mixer, beat together the cream cheese, confectioners' sugar, and vanilla until light and fluffy, about 2 minutes. Spread the frosting over the cake, cut the cake into slices, and serve.

BREAKIN' IT DOWN

	Before	After
Fat	16g	7g
Calories	311	199

5g protein | 30g carbohydrate
1g fiber | 344mg sodium

Bittersweet Chocolate Cheesecake

You may be wondering how a mere nine-inch cake feeds a crowd of sixteen. But I promise you, folks, once you sample the decadent richness of this chocolate cheesecake, you will understand how a thin slice is more than enough to satisfy even the chocoholic's biggest craving. **Serves 16**

1 cup finely crushed chocolate wafer cookies

2 tablespoons plus ⅔ cup sugar

2 tablespoons unsalted butter, melted

12 ounces bittersweet chocolate chips

2 packages (8 ounces each) fat-free cream cheese (or use low-fat; optional), softened

1 package (8 ounces) low-fat cream cheese (Neufchâtel), softened

¼ teaspoon salt

3 large eggs

1 cup fat-free Greek yogurt (or use low-fat; optional)

2 teaspoons pure vanilla extract

Fat-free whipped topping (or use light; optional), thawed, for serving

1. Preheat the oven to 350°F. Spray a 9-inch springform pan lightly with cooking spray.

2. In a small bowl, combine the cookies, 2 tablespoons of the sugar, and the butter. Press the mixture into the bottom of the prepared pan.

3. In a small microwave-safe bowl, heat the chocolate in the microwave on medium heat for 10-second intervals, stirring between each round, until the chocolate is melted and smooth.

4. In the bowl of an electric mixer fitted with the paddle attachment, or using a handheld mixer, beat together the cream cheeses, the remaining ⅔ cup sugar, melted chocolate, and salt. Beat in the eggs, one at a time, until combined, then beat in the yogurt and vanilla.

5. Pour the batter into the prepared crust. Bake for about 1 hour, or until the filling is almost set. Cool completely on a wire rack at room temperature, then place in the refrigerator to chill for 1 hour. Gently remove from the springform pan and serve, with whipped topping dolloped on top.

BREAKIN' IT DOWN

	Before	After
Fat	38g	12g
Calories	562	248

9g protein | 29g carbohydrate
2g fiber | 311mg sodium

Nutritional count does not include whipped topping for serving.

A Clean Cut

Here's a trick for cutting a clean slice of cheesecake. Use a hot, dry knife that has been heated up under running water, then wiped dry with a kitchen towel. Repeat heating and drying knife between every two slices and your wedges will come out nice and clean without sticking to the knife.

Angel Food Cake with Devil Sauce

This dessert manages to be light and airy at the same time as it is rich and decadent. I swear that this angel food cake positively floats on the plate. And for me, the cake is enough of a dessert to satisfy my sweet craving. But for most people I know, it's the sauce that makes them sit up and take notice: creamy, chocolaty, and sinful tasting. **Serves 10 / Makes 1¼ cups sauce**

Cake

1 cup sifted cake flour

1¼ cups superfine sugar

1½ cups egg whites (from about 12 large eggs), at room temperature

2 teaspoons pure vanilla extract

1 teaspoon cream of tartar

¼ teaspoon salt

Sauce

½ cup semisweet chocolate chips

½ cup 1% milk

1 tablespoon unsweetened cocoa powder

1 tablespoon granulated sugar

⅛ teaspoon pure vanilla extract

½ cup low-fat sour cream

1. To make the cake: Preheat the oven to 375°F and position a rack in the lower third of the oven.

2. Over a medium bowl, sift the flour with ¼ cup of the superfine sugar.

3. In the bowl of an electric mixer fitted with the whisk attachment, or using a handheld mixer, combine the egg whites with 1 tablespoon warm water and beat on high speed until frothy. Add the vanilla, cream of tartar, and salt and continue beating until soft peaks form. Gradually beat in the remaining 1 cup superfine sugar, 2 tablespoons at a time. Continue beating on high speed until stiff peaks form.

4. Sift one-third of the flour mixture over the beaten egg whites and, using a rubber spatula, gently fold in. Repeat two times with the remaining flour mixture.

5. Pour the batter into an ungreased tube pan. Drop the pan lightly on the counter to release any big air bubbles and smooth the top.

6. Bake for about 30 minutes, or until the top is golden and a wooden skewer inserted into the cake comes out clean.

7. Meanwhile, to make the sauce: In a small saucepan over medium heat, combine the chocolate chips, milk, cocoa powder, and granulated sugar. Stir until the chocolate is completely melted and the mixture is smooth. (To be extra careful the chocolate doesn't overheat, you can melt it in a double boiler instead. Just pour the chocolate chips, milk, cocoa powder, and granulated sugar into a saucepan and place over another saucepan of simmering water, making sure the water does not touch the bottom of the chocolate

BREAKIN' IT DOWN

	Before	After
Fat	24g	5g
Calories	429	235

7g protein | 43g carbohydrate
1g fiber | 140mg sodium

(continued)

pan. Stir until the chocolate is completely melted and the mixture is smooth.) Stir in the vanilla, then pour the chocolate into a medium bowl to cool to room temperature. Once cooled, whisk in the sour cream until smooth.

8. Place the cake on a wire rack and let cool completely in the pan, at least 1 hour. When the cake has cooled, run a long, thin knife along the edges of the pan to release the cake. Invert onto the wire rack, then invert again onto a cake plate. Slice the angel food cake and serve drizzled with the rich devil sauce.

The Soft Touch

The secret to this cake's incredible lightness is in the whipped egg whites. You want to handle the egg whites gently so that you don't knock out the air that you whipped into them. Be careful to use a gentle lifting motion with your rubber spatula when you fold in the flour. All that trapped-in air translates to a lighter-than-clouds cake.

Doughnut Bread Pudding

I love to serve this bread pudding when I'm having a large group over for brunch. It's a surefire crowd-pleaser, I tell you. But, doughnuts aren't just for breakfast. This pudding also makes a fine end to a casual family dinner. **Serves 10**

1. Preheat the oven to 400°F.

2. Spread the doughnut pieces on a rimmed baking sheet and toast until golden and dry to the touch, about 10 minutes.

3. Reduce the oven temperature to 350°F. Spray a 9 by 13-inch baking dish with cooking spray.

4. In a large bowl, whisk together the eggs, egg whites, half-and-half, brown sugar, rum (if using), cinnamon, and salt. Stir in the pineapples and raisins.

5. Spread the doughnut pieces into the bottom of the prepared baking dish. Pour the custard mixture over the doughnuts. Bake for 40 to 50 minutes, until golden and firm to the touch. Let the bread pudding cool for 10 minutes, then sprinkle with the cherries and serve.

12 ounces plain cake doughnuts, broken into 1-inch chunks

2 large eggs, lightly beaten

2 large egg whites, lightly beaten

1½ cups fat-free half-and-half (or use low-fat; optional)

¼ cup packed light brown sugar

2 tablespoons dark rum (optional)

1 teaspoon ground cinnamon

Pinch of salt

½ cup finely chopped fresh or canned pineapples, drained if canned

¼ cup raisins

3 tablespoons coarsely chopped maraschino cherries

Doughnut Whole

When I can get my hands on them, I like to use whole-wheat doughnuts in this bread pudding. They taste great and are better for you than those made from white flour.

BREAKIN' IT DOWN

	Before	After
Fat	16g	10g
Calories	470	206

5g protein | 2g carbohydrate
0g fiber | 263mg sodium

Chocolate Marshmallow Mousse

I certainly do fondly remember the good old Fluffernutter sandwiches of my school days: a slathering of peanut butter, topped with a healthy dollop of Marshmallow Fluff, sandwiched between two slices of soft white bread. It has to be one of the most American of sandwiches. In this recipe, I've found a new and modern way to use Marshmallow Fluff. In this mousse it lends its light and creamy texture to what seems like a decadent treat. It's pure chocolate marshmallow heaven. **Serves 6**

1 package (3.4 ounces) chocolate pudding mix (not instant)

2 cups 2% milk

¾ cup Marshmallow Fluff

Fat-free whipped topping (or use light; optional), thawed, for serving

In a medium saucepan, combine the pudding mix and milk and bring to a boil over medium heat, stirring constantly. As soon as the mixture reaches a boil, turn off the heat and whisk in the Marshmallow Fluff. Divide the mixture among six dessert cups and refrigerate until cool. Top each with a dollop of whipped topping before serving.

BREAKIN' IT DOWN

	Before	After
Fat	43g	2g
Calories	480	159

3g protein | 32g carbohydrate
0g fiber | 110mg sodium

Boil Over

Be sure to keep a close eye on the milk when you are heating it up. Milk has a way of surprising you when it reaches a boil. Once it hits that boil, it's up over the pan and all over your stove top in no time flat. As soon as you see some bubbling movement, take it off the heat and get that Marshmallow Fluff in.

Savannah Tiramisù

This totally decadent tiramisù is a must-have in your dinner party arsenal of desserts. I like to serve it in individual dessert goblets—it lets you see all the pretty layers and has the extra advantage of built-in portion control! **Serves 8**

1. Prepare the pudding with the milk according to the package directions. Stir in the bourbon and refrigerate until cool.

2. Divide half of the ladyfingers among eight dessert glasses. Create four more layers over the ladyfingers by dividing half of the pudding, half of the whipped topping, half of the pecans, and half of the coconut among the eight glasses. Then repeat the layers with the remaining ingredients, ending with the pecans and coconut. You can prepare your tiramisùs the day before and let them sit, loosely covered, in the fridge.

1 package (3 ounces) vanilla pudding mix (not instant)

2 cups 2% milk

3 tablespoons bourbon or rum

1 package (3 ounces/24 ladyfingers) soft ladyfingers, torn into bite-size pieces

2¼ cups chocolate whipped topping

½ cup pecans, toasted and coarsely chopped

¼ cup shredded coconut, toasted

Ladyfingers

Like any traditional tiramisù, these are made with ladyfinger cookies. You can find ladyfingers in the cookie section of the supermarket.

BREAKIN' IT DOWN

	Before	After
Fat	32g	12g
Calories	600	295

5g protein | 38g carbohydrate
2g fiber | 136mg sodium

Peach Cobbler

Cobblers come in many different varieties. This one features big dollops of crusty biscuit that pair so nicely with the cinnamon-laced peaches. Top this off with a nice scoop of vanilla gelato (a leaner version of ice cream) or frozen yogurt and you've got yourself one heck of a finish to your meal. **Serves 8**

5 cups sliced fresh or frozen peaches, unpeeled if fresh, thawed and drained if frozen

3 tablespoons plus ⅓ cup packed light brown sugar

1 tablespoon plus 1 cup all-purpose flour

2 teaspoons fresh lemon juice

¼ teaspoon ground cinnamon

1 teaspoon baking powder

½ teaspoon salt

5 tablespoons cold unsalted butter, cut into small pieces

1. Preheat the oven to 425°F.

2. In a large bowl, toss together the peaches, 3 tablespoons of the brown sugar, 1 tablespoon of the flour, the lemon juice, and cinnamon. Spoon the mixture into a 2-quart baking dish and bake for 10 minutes.

3. Meanwhile, in a medium bowl, whisk together the remaining ⅓ cup sugar, the remaining 1 cup flour, the baking powder, and salt. Cut in the butter with a fork until the mixture resembles coarse meal. Stir in ¼ cup boiling water and mix just until the dough comes together.

4. Spoon dollops of dough over the baked peaches. Return the cobbler to the oven and bake for about 25 minutes, until bubbling and golden brown. Let the cobbler cool slightly before serving.

BREAKIN' IT DOWN

	Before	After
Fat	14g	8g
Calories	437	216

2g protein | 36g carbohydrate
2g fiber | 202mg sodium

Do Your Chores

Do you know that an hour of gardening can burn as many as 250 calories? Household chores like mopping, dusting, and raking the leaves are great ways to burn calories while you get things done.

It IS My Mama's Peach Cake

I have to give credit where credit is due. I made so few changes to this cake that it's still Mama's cake through and through. Oh, I lightened it up here and there, but this classic is so good as is and so surprisingly healthy as my Mama makes it, I figured, "Why mess with success?" **Serves 12 to 16**

1 container (6 ounces) fat-free peach yogurt (or use low-fat; optional)

1 container (8 ounces) fat-free whipped topping (or use light; optional), thawed

2 cups all-purpose flour

2 teaspoons baking powder

1 teaspoon ground cinnamon

1 teaspoon salt

½ teaspoon baking soda

1½ cups sugar

1 can (15 ounces) sliced peaches in juice, drained

½ cup canola oil

3 large egg whites

1 teaspoon pure vanilla extract

½ cup 2% buttermilk

1. Preheat the oven to 350°F. Spray a Bundt pan with baking spray (the kind containing flour).

2. In a medium bowl, fold the yogurt into the whipped topping until combined. Refrigerate until ready to use.

3. In a separate medium bowl, whisk together the flour, baking powder, cinnamon, salt, and baking soda. In the bowl of an electric mixer fitted with the paddle attachment, or using a handheld mixer, beat the sugar, peaches, oil, egg whites, and vanilla on medium-high speed until the peaches are pureed. With the mixer on low, beat in half of the flour mixture, followed by the buttermilk, then the remaining flour mixture. Beat until just combined.

4. Pour the batter into the prepared pan and bake for 45 to 50 minutes, until a toothpick inserted into the center of the cake comes out clean. Let the cake cool on a wire rack for 10 minutes. Then turn it out onto the wire rack to cool completely before frosting with the yogurt and whipped topping mixture.

BREAKIN' IT DOWN

	Before	After
Fat	17g	8g
Calories	306	273

4g protein | 46g carbohydrate
1g fiber | 301mg sodium

Nutritional count based on 14 servings

Cool It

Before frosting cakes, make sure you cool them completely. This way the cake sets and you won't get little crumbs from the cake coming off in your frosting. Also, a hot cake can melt the frosting as you're spreading it on, and that is not a good look for a cake.

Strawberry Streusel Cake

Unlike most streusel-topped cakes, which can be dense, this cake is so light and fluffy it feels as if it's made from air. And that's my kind of dessert. I like a dessert that gives me something sweet to finish my meal with or to enjoy next to a cup of coffee, but does not make me feel overly full. **Serves 10**

1. Preheat the oven to 350°F. Spray a 9-inch round cake pan with cooking spray.

2. In a medium bowl, whisk together 1⅓ cups of the flour, the baking powder, baking soda, and salt. In a separate medium bowl, whisk together the yogurt, 3 tablespoons of the butter, ⅔ cup of the sugar, the egg, and vanilla. Whisk the yogurt mixture into the flour mixture. Using a rubber spatula, fold in the strawberries. Scrape the batter into the prepared pan.

3. In a small bowl, use your fingers to rub together the remaining 3 tablespoons flour, the remaining 2 tablespoons sugar, the remaining 1 tablespoon melted butter, and the cinnamon. Sprinkle over the top of the cake. Bake for 40 to 50 minutes, until golden brown and a toothpick inserted into the center comes out clean. Let the cake cool on a wire rack before serving.

1⅓ cups plus 3 tablespoons all-purpose flour

1 teaspoon baking powder

¼ teaspoon baking soda

¼ teaspoon salt

¾ cup 2% Greek yogurt

4 tablespoons (½ stick) unsalted butter, melted

⅔ cup plus 2 tablespoons sugar

1 large egg

1 teaspoon pure vanilla extract

1 cup finely chopped fresh or thawed frozen strawberries

1 teaspoon ground cinnamon

Subs 'n Swaps
This cake is also sensational with fresh or frozen blueberries or raspberries in place of the strawberries.

BREAKIN' IT DOWN

	Before	After
Fat	17g	1g
Calories	342	155

4g protein | 32g carbohydrate
1g fiber | 140mg sodium

LUSCIOUS DESSERTS

181

White Chocolate–Peppermint Popcorn Balls

Popcorn balls are made all throughout the South during the month of December. They're a festive way to get the kids involved in whipping up holiday treats. I like to play around with this recipe. Sometimes I give these fun popcorn balls a sweet and savory taste by adding some salt to my popcorn. It tastes great paired with the super-sweet white chocolate. And if you're not a peppermint fan, feel free to swap in vanilla or almond extract instead. **Makes 10 balls**

¼ cup low-calorie butter substitute stick or spread

1 bag (10½ ounces) mini marshmallows

¼ teaspoon peppermint extract

⅓ cup white chocolate chips

10 cups air-popped popcorn

1. In a medium saucepan, melt the butter substitute over medium heat. Add the marshmallows, reduce the heat to medium-low, and stir until the marshmallows are melted. Remove from the heat and stir in the peppermint extract and the white chocolate chips. Continue stirring until the chips are melted.

2. Spray a large bowl lightly with cooking spray and add the popcorn. Pour the marshmallow mixture over the top and stir with a wooden spoon until the popcorn is evenly coated.

3. Using hands that have been greased with a little vegetable oil, shape the popcorn mixture into 10 balls, transferring them to a waxed paper–lined rimmed baking sheet as you go. Let the balls cool for 15 minutes before serving.

BREAKIN' IT DOWN

	Before	After
Fat	24g	3g
Calories	562	176

2g protein | 3g carbohydrate
1g fiber | 63mg sodium

Nutritional count per ball

Sticky Situation

Here's a tip for dealing with the sticky popcorn mix. Spray a 1-cup measuring cup with cooking spray and use it to scoop out your portions of popcorn. This way you won't need to dig your hands into the popcorn and get it stuck all over you.

Piña Colada Granita

Granitas are an easier-to-fix version of sorbet. They are partially frozen and have a coarser texture because you don't churn them in an ice cream maker. In fact, all you need to make a granita are water, a sweetener, flavorings, a shallow pan, and a fork. This granita is more than just a dessert. Add a shot of rum, and you've got yourself a mighty refreshing frozen cocktail. I like to make the granita and add the rum by pouring it over when I serve it at the table. It's like sippin' a little piece of summer. **Serves 8**

1 can (20 ounces) crushed pineapple with juice

1 can (15 ounces) light coconut milk

2 tablespoons honey

Juice of ½ lime

Pinch of salt

½ cup unsweetened coconut flakes

1. In a blender, puree the pineapple and its juice, the coconut milk, honey, lime juice, and salt until smooth. Pour into a wide, shallow plastic or metal container. Freeze, stirring and breaking up any frozen chunks with a fork every 30 minutes, until the granita is frozen but easy to scoop, about 2 hours.

2. Meanwhile, preheat the oven to 325°F.

3. Spread the coconut flakes on a rimmed baking sheet and toast until golden, 5 to 10 minutes. Check the coconut flakes frequently as they brown quickly. Cool to room temperature.

4. Sprinkle 1 tablespoon of the toasted coconut over each serving of granita.

BREAKIN' IT DOWN

	Before	After
Fat	27g	6g
Calories	442	117

1g protein | 17g carbohydrate
1g fiber | 90mg sodium

Even Freezin'

To speed up the freezing time of this granita, use the widest, shallowest pan you can fit in your freezer. And make sure the pan is placed level in your freezer so that you get even freezing throughout.

CHAPTER 10

Menus, Tricks, and Tips

FOR THOSE LOOKING TO DROP a few pounds, the following is a week's worth of 1,500 calories or fewer recipes (breakfast, lunch, dinner, and dessert or snack) that work for tightening your waistline without sacrificing flavor.

Sunday (1,489 CALORIES)

Breakfast (296): **Pecan Waffles with Strawberry Syrup** (page 160)

Lunch (399): **Southern Tomato Sandwiches** (151) (page 112) **and Confederate Bean Soup** (248) (page 34)

Dinner (677): **Shore Is Good Seafood Dip** (94) (page 9) **with ½ cup carrot sticks and ½ cup celery sticks for dipping** (34), **Sunday Roast Chicken** (349) (page 55) **with Oven Cheese Fries** (107) (page 131) **and Creamed Spinach** (93) (page 122)

Dessert (117): **Piña Colada Granita** (page 184)

Monday (1,322 CALORIES)

Breakfast (299): **Maple Ham Biscuits (180)** (page 148) **with 1 large hard-boiled egg** (78) **and ½ grapefruit** (41)

Lunch (380): **Crispy, Crunchy Reubens (168)** (page 108) **with 1 cup Jack's Corn Chowder (131)** (page 28) **and a small pear** (81)

Snack (338): **2 ounces dry-roasted salted almonds**

Dinner (305): **Monday-Night Red Beans and Rice (273)** (page 97) **with Quick Pickled Cucumbers** (32) (page 142)

Tuesday (1,431 CALORIES)

Breakfast (480): **Warm-You-Up Cinnamon Streusel Oatmeal (280)** (page 151) **and 1 cup sliced banana** (200)

Lunch (388): **Chicken Salad with a Twist in lettuce wraps (196)** (page 117) **and French Onion Soup (192)** (page 30)

Snack (175): **1 small apple** (55) **and ½ cup finely chopped low-fat Swiss cheese** (120)

Dinner (388): **Barbecue-Style Pork Chops (239)** (page 70) **with Baked Sweet Potato Fries (105)** (page 132) **and 1 cup steamed green beans** (44)

Wednesday (1,242 CALORIES)

Breakfast (281): **Easy Eggs Florentine** (page 156)

Lunch (351): **Rotelle Pasta Salad with Garlicky Broccoli and Mozzarella** (210) (page 50) **and Secret Ingredient Butternut Squash Soup** (141) (page 25)

Snack (135): **1 container low-fat strawberry yogurt**

Dinner (227): **Cheeseburger Casserole** (193) (page 85) **and 1 cup cherry tomato salad** (27) **with 1 tablespoon fat-free dressing** (7)

Dessert (248): **Bittersweet Chocolate Cheesecake** (page 170)

Thursday (1,313 CALORIES)

Breakfast (299): **Toasted-Waffle Ham and Egg Sandwich** (246) (page 158) **with 1 cup sliced strawberries** (53)

Lunch (272): **Caesar Salad** (152) (page 44) **with 4-ounce grilled boneless, skinless chicken breast** (120)

Snack (96): **1 cup sliced red bell peppers** (24) **with 3 tablespoons fat-free ranch dressing for dipping** (72)

Dinner (412): **Turkey Marsala** (250) (page 62) **with ½ cup cooked brown rice** (108) **and 1 cup boiled chopped broccoli** (54)

Late-Night Snack (234): **2 cups air-popped popcorn** (16) **and 1 bar (1½ ounces) dark chocolate** (218)

Friday (1,380 CALORIES)

Breakfast (226): **Good Morning Pumpkin-Corn Muffins** (161) (page 149) **and 1 small orange** (65)

Lunch (482): **Avocado BLT** (334) (page 110) **and 20 baked tortilla chips** (148)

Snack (105): **1 chocolate chip granola bar**

Dinner (332): **Chicken and Dumplings** (309) (page 92) **with a green salad (2 cups lettuce and 1 tablespoon fat-free dressing)** (23)

Dessert (235): **Angel Food Cake with Devil Sauce** (page 172)

Saturday (1,408 CALORIES)

Breakfast (282): **Tomato Grits and Sausage** (170) (page 152) **with a slice of Real Southern Corn Bread** (112) (page 134)

Lunch (520): **The Son's Beef Vegetable Soup** (322) (page 31) **and Spinach Salad with Warm Bacon Dressing** (198) (page 40)

Dinner (439): **Gather Round Artichoke and Spinach Dip** (86) (page 10) **with 6 fat-free low-sodium saltines for dipping** (118), **Memphis Dry Rub Shrimp Skewers** (105) (page 78), **and Succotash** (130) (page 138)

Dessert (167): **Raspberry Angel Pie** (page 166)

Seven Healthy Activities and Tips

BEING HEALTHY IS NOT JUST about eating right. You've got to get out there and exercise if you want to keep it all in balance. Luckily that doesn't have to mean pumping iron and running marathons. There are all sorts of ways you can work exercise into your everyday life without too much of an impact on your day-to-day routine. But finding the time is only half the battle when it comes to exercise. The other half is finding the motivation. Fear not, folks, I've got a few little tricks up my sleeve for helping you solve both of these issues. These seven handy hints will help you get the right balance between eating right and getting your body on the move.

1. Walk more and drive less. You say you don't have enough time to exercise? Well, here's a way to work some exercise into your daily errand routine. When I head out to the supermarket, I try to park in the farthest-away parking space in the lot. That walk to and from the market door provides me with another opportunity to exercise. And in my busy schedule, I've got to take every opportunity I can find!

2. Find yourself a friend to share your exercise routine with. Going to the gym or for a run or walk with a friend is the best motivation. I know that I look forward to the kinship I feel when I meet my coach and good friend Sam for a workout session. But besides all that, it's just that much harder to cancel out on a visit to the gym when you know someone is waiting for you there.

3. Drink water. It's as simple as that. Our bodies need water to perform, and they need plenty of it. You won't have the energy you need to get your body moving if it isn't properly hydrated. I like to start right as soon as I wake up. I love a good cup of coffee in the morning just as much as the next guy, but first I get myself a big glass of water, sometimes with a little lemon in it. This helps to get my metabolism going and wakes up my muscles for the day. Then I make sure I have at least eight cups of water throughout the rest of my day. It's one of the best things you can do for your body, and it's so darn easy.

4. Use the stairs as often as you can. Bounding up a flight of stairs to get where you're going is a great way to work in some cardiovascular exercise. On your way in to work, skip the elevator and hoof it up to your office. Or, at the mall, take a pass on the escalator and use the stairs. It may not seem like much, but these little changes to your daily routine will make a big difference.

5. Go dancing. Now, you guys out there may prefer to watch the big game on television, but sometimes you've got to take one for the team and take your lady out dancing. Not only will you make your partner happy, but you'll also be sneaking in a great cardio workout for the two of you. I'm telling you, it's a win-win situation.

6. Take an evening walk, especially after a hearty meal. What you don't want to do after dinner is sit yourself on the couch for the remainder of the evening. A walk out under the stars helps to get your metabolism going to work off the little indulgences of the day.

7. Keep an eye on your portion sizes. If you practice portion control, you'll find that you can eat almost anything you want. Don't deprive yourself. By all means enjoy your desserts now and again; just make sure you enjoy them in moderation. You see, while food gives the body energy to exercise, *too much* food will actually have the reverse effect. Overeating saps the body of the will to move. To help you out with portion control, each recipe in my book provides detailed nutritional analysis per serving.

Five Party Menus to Keep Your Diet on Track, Even When You Are Celebrating

THINK WE CAN ALL AGREE that parties are not the easiest places to eat right. It can be downright dangerous being surrounded by all the tasty treats friends set out to welcome you. But if I have any say in the matter, I like to keep things entertaining *and* healthy. It really doesn't take much to cut out the extra calories and still put food on the table that friends and family want to dig in to. To help you out with these occasions, I've created some menus using the recipes you'll find right here in my book.

Party at the Grill

Grilling season is long in my house, so I've got a whole arsenal of barbecue menus. This one, though, is quintessential Bobby. Pickled shrimp, a juicy steak, and a lighter-than-air raspberry pie, all meant to be eaten outside in the fresh air. And my Piña Colada Granita is a great finish to a great meal when you top it off with a shot of rum. I say, cheers to that, folks!

Pickled Shrimp (page 6)

The Lady & Sons Wedge Salad with Blue Cheese and Bacon (page 39)

Grilled Filet Mignon with Vidalia Onions (page 64)

Mediterranean Grilled Veggies (page 124)

Raspberry Angel Pie (page 166)

Piña Colada Granita (page 184)

Brunch

When I have folks over for brunch, I like to serve dishes that I can make up ahead of time so that I'm not too crazed in the morning. That's why I usually set out a bake of some sort or another. Paired with some delicious wraps and sandwiches, it's the perfect mix of lunch and breakfast.

Bobby's Turkey and Cheese Power Wrap (page 109)

Southern Tomato Sandwiches (page 112)

Western Omelet Bake (page 155)

Doughnut Bread Pudding (page 175)

Date Night

Even if you're not from the South, I think this menu makes for a special night in. Share it with someone special.

Mini Savannah Crab Cakes (page 14)

Spinach Salad with Warm Bacon Dressing (page 40)

Charleston Shrimp and Grits (page 74)

Savannah Tiramisù (page 177)

Family Dinner

When I have my family over, no matter what the occasion, I like it to feel like a holiday. And since my favorite holiday is Thanksgiving, that's the food I like to riff off. This menu whips up a delicious and leaner Southern Thanksgiving feast.

Game-Day TV Party

Having the guys over to watch the big game demands a simple menu that can be eaten on the couch in front of the television. For these occasions, I like to go with food you can eat with your hands. That's why sandwiches are a great choice for this type of get-together. And sandwiches packed full of meat, well, they're bound to be a hit.

Tailgate Party

A good tailgate menu is essential in my life. I spend so many weekends during college football season hanging out with friends before the big game. We throw the ball around, have a couple beers, and get ourselves pumped up for the game. This menu features easy, do-ahead dishes that are tailor made to take on the go. I guarantee that it will get your game-day spirit on without a whole lot of extra work and without a whole lot of extra calories. Go, Dawgs!

It's a Party Guacamole (page 8)

New-fashioned Cabbage Slaw (page 42)

Mexican Fiesta Casserole (page 94)

Gooey Less-Butter Cake (page 164)

Stocking the Healthy Pantry, Fridge, and Freezer

WHEN I FIRST DECIDED TO commit myself to a healthy lifestyle make-over, I found that the easier I made it for myself to make the right food decisions, the more successful I was. And key to that goal was building a pantry, fridge, and freezer that were stocked with the ingredients for creating delicious meals that were leaner and lighter. Out went the bags of chips and cartons of cream and in came an array of simple and delicious foods for building meals that would keep me satisfied and fit. I found that all the ingredients I needed, or that you will need, were readily available at the supermarket. With these ingredients at your fingertips, you'll see that it's just as fast and easy to whip up your own fresh meals at home as it is to drive to the take-out counter. And I guarantee you'll feel a whole lot better enjoying a meal that you've made yourself over anything you can eat out of a Styrofoam carton.

In the Pantry

Baking

Baking mix, whole-wheat

Baking powder

Baking soda

Chocolate—dark, milk, and white

Cocoa powder

Coconut—flaked and shredded

Cream of tartar

Cornmeal

Cornstarch

Flour—all-purpose and whole-wheat

Muffin mix

Sugar—brown, confectioners', granulated, and superfine

Vanilla extract, pure

Yellow cake mix, packaged

Broths and Soups

Beef, low-sodium

Chicken, low-sodium

Cream of chicken soup, low-fat and low-sodium

Cream of mushroom soup, low-fat and low-sodium

Vegetable, low-sodium

Beans, Fruits, and Vegetables (canned)

Black beans

Black-eyed peas

Chickpeas

Corn—creamed and kernel

Kidney beans

Peaches

Pineapple—crushed and rings

Water chestnuts

White beans

Condiments

Honey

Ketchup

Oil—canola, olive, and cooking spray

Soy sauce, low-sodium

Vinegar—apple cider, balsamic, red and white wine

Worcestershire sauce

Fish (canned)

Crabmeat

Salmon, water-packed

Tuna, water-packed

Fruits and Vegetables

Apples

Bananas

Butternut squash

Garlic

Lemons

Limes

Onions—red, sweet, and yellow

Oranges

Potatoes—sweet and white

Miscellaneous

Air-popped popcorn

Coconut milk, light

Corn flakes

Evaporated milk—fat-free and 2%

Gelatin mix

Marshmallows—mini and Marshmallow Fluff

Nuts—pecans, walnuts, peanuts

Oats—instant and rolled

Peanut butter

Pudding mix

Raisins

Salsa (jarred)

Taco seasoning packets

Pastas, Rice, Bread, and Grains

Bread—whole-wheat and white

Bread crumbs—dried and Japanese panko

Grits, quick-cooking

Pastas—whole-grain and white flour in different shapes and sizes

Rice—brown and white

Tortillas—corn, whole-wheat, and flour

Wraps—whole-wheat and low-carb

Tomatoes (canned)

Crushed

Diced, low-sodium, plain or with chiles

Paste

Sauce

Whole

Spices

Bay leaves

Black pepper

Cajun seasoning

Cayenne pepper

Crab boil
Crushed red pepper flakes
Dried basil
Dried Italian seasoning
Dried marjoram
Dried minced garlic
Dried minced onion
Dried oregano
Dried parsley flakes
Dried rosemary
Dried thyme
Dry mustard powder
Garlic powder
Ground cinnamon
Ground coriander
Ground cumin
Ground nutmeg
Onion powder
Paula Deen House Seasoning
Salt—coarse sea salt

In the Fridge

Condiments, Jarred Foods, and Miscellaneous

Applesauce
Artichoke hearts
Barbecue sauce
Chutney
Eggs, large
Hot sauce—Sriracha, Tabasco, etc.
Maple syrup, light
Mustard—Dijon, honey, spicy brown, yellow, whole-grain, etc.
Pickled vegetables—dill cucumbers, jalapeños, okra, relish, pimientos, sauerkraut, yellow pepper rings, etc.

Tahini
Tofu

Dairy

Butter—unsalted, low-calorie butter substitute (spread and stick)
Buttermilk—1% and 2%
Cheese—blue cheese, low-fat Cheddar, low-fat feta, light garlic and herb spread, low-fat Italian and Mexican cheese blends, low-fat Monterey Jack, part-skim mozzarella, low-fat pepper Jack, low-fat Swiss, Parmesan, and fat-free ricotta
Cottage cheese, low-fat
Cream cheese—fat-free and low-fat, whipped and bar
Greek yogurt—fat-free, low-fat, and 2%
Half-and-half—fat-free and low-fat
Mayonnaise—fat-free and light
Milk—1%, 2%, and skim
Sour cream—fat-free and low-fat

Fish and Seafood

Crabmeat, lump
Dark-meat fish—salmon, tuna, etc.
Scallops
Shrimp
White-meat fish—grouper, tilapia, etc.

Fruits and Vegetables

Avocados
Bell peppers
Berries
Broccoli
Carrots
Celery
Coleslaw mix

Corn on the cob

Cucumbers

Eggplants

Grapes

Green beans

Hot chile peppers

Lettuce, bagged and heads

Mushrooms—white, cremini, etc.

Okra

Scallions

Spinach and other dark leafy greens, such as collards

Tomatoes

Yellow squash

Zucchini

Herbs (fresh)

Basil

Chives

Cilantro

Dill

Oregano

Parsley

Rosemary

Sage

Thyme

Meat (freeze for longer storage)

Bacon—Canadian, pork, and turkey

Beef—boneless chuck, cube steak, lean ground, and tenderloin

Chicken—boneless, skinless breasts and thighs; ground; sausage; and whole roasters

Deli meats—fat-free and low-sodium turkey, ham, and roast beef

Ham, lean steaks

Pork—chops, ribs, shoulder, and tenderloin

Turkey—boneless breast, cutlets, ground, sausages, and smoked neck or wing

In the Freezer

Berries

Black-eyed peas

Butter beans

Corn

Lima beans

Mixed vegetables

Okra

Pie shells, whole-wheat

Peaches

Peas

Spinach

Waffles, whole-grain

Whipped topping—chocolate, fat-free, and light

Healthy Subs and Swaps

WHILE MY DIET HAS CHANGED in a big way, there are some dishes I refuse to give up. Case in point: fried chicken. As a good Southern boy, I'd be lost without fried chicken in my life in some form or another. For my un-give-up-able dishes, I had to find ways to swap out the big fat and calorie offenders for some healthier alternatives. These swaps are the key to eating right without depriving myself of the dishes I've always loved most. I'd like to share with you some of my most successful healthy subs and swaps. These are low-fat, low-calorie ingredients that act as stand-ins for full-fat alternatives but still deliver delicious, authentic-tasting dishes.

Applesauce

Applesauce is a healthy staple in my fridge. It's an awesome tool in the fight to cut fat. It keeps casseroles moist without changing the flavor and it's a fantastic substitute for oil. You'll have good success swapping out oil for applesauce in most baking recipes.

Buttermilk

I simply can't do without buttermilk. But while I used to keep a carton in my fridge for fried chicken and pancake cravings, I now keep one in the fridge as my low-fat substitute for whole milk, cream, and sour cream. Buttermilk works like a dream in baked goods and is a great base for creamy salad dressings. It's also what we Southerners dip our fried foods into before dredging them in a dry coating. In the past, I wouldn't dream of frying up okra, chicken, or green tomatoes without first marinating them in buttermilk. And even though I'm doing more oven roasting than deep-frying these days, I still never skip the buttermilk marinade.

Egg White/Whole Egg Mixture

When a dish calls for whole eggs, I swap in a mix of egg whites and whole eggs, going heavier on the whites than the yolks. The way I see it, the egg white is the best part of the egg. Egg whites are packed with protein and contain no fat or cholesterol. But don't go throwing the yolks out with the trash. While they do contain fat and cholesterol, they also provide a lot of nutritional value, such as calcium, iron, and potassium.

Fat-Free Frozen Yogurt

Some desserts just scream out for a scoop of ice cream on top. Fat-free frozen yogurt does the trick instead. And because yogurt has more protein than heavy cream, it's better for you in more ways than one.

Fat-Free or 2% Greek Yogurt

If you haven't discovered Greek yogurt yet, let me be the one to sing its praises. I always have a tub in my fridge. It's such a versatile ingredient, good for desserts, dressings, and garnishes alike. You can use it pretty much anywhere you'd use sour cream or mayonnaise and still achieve a nice creamy texture without the extra fat. As a bonus, it just happens to be loaded with protein and calcium.

Japanese Panko and Corn Flakes

With these two ingredients in my pantry, I can give my food an authentically textured "fried" coating even when I'm oven roasting. If it's Crunchy Fried Chicken or Chicken-Fried Steak with Cream Gravy that I'm putting together, crushed corn flakes is what I reach for every time. For crunchy toppings on casseroles or a hearty coating on vegetables, panko is the way to go.

Low-Sodium Broth and Unsalted Butter

High-sodium packaged broths and salted butter are in the past for me. Now I use low-sodium broth and unsalted butter in all my dishes. That way, I'm in control of how much salt goes into my meal. Remember, you can always add salt to your dish if you think it needs it, but you can't take it out once it's been added.

Spray Oil

Cooking spray is a great way to cut calories, fat, and cholesterol in your food. I always have a can or two in my kitchen. And you'll find there are all sorts of different varieties out there, from olive oil to canola to grape seed oil. They provide the same nonstick surface as oil or butter without making your food greasy.

Turkey

I've made a real effort to cut down on the amount of beef I eat. During the workweek, I mostly turn to fish, fowl, and lots of veggies. And when I'm cooking up a dish that I used to make with ground beef, I either cut the beef amount in half and swap in ground turkey for the balance or sub in ground turkey entirely. I'm telling you, I find I don't miss the beef at all. It really doesn't get much leaner than turkey.

Whole-Wheat Bread, Flour, Pasta, and Brown Rice

It's as simple as this: The complex carbohydrates found in whole grains are better for you than the refined carbohydrates in milled (or white) grains. Brown breads, pastas, and rice are the right choices over white bread, pasta, and rice. You see, the process of refining the white grain–based foods strips them of key vitamins and minerals that are native to the whole grains. As often as you can, choose whole grains over refined grains, and I guarantee you'll see and feel a difference in your body.

Wraps

When it comes to sandwiches, wraps are a great alternative to bread, especially if you're watching your carbs. There are so many different flavors and varieties of wraps out there, from sun-dried tomato and garlic to multigrain and reduced carb. Why, there's so much choice out there that I can do the same sandwich a few times a week using different wraps and it will taste different each and every time.

Bobby's Fantastic Fourteen

HERE'S A SELECT GROUP OF foods that I try to work into my diet as often as possible. You may have heard them referred to as superfoods, but I've dubbed them my Fantastic Fourteen. These fourteen foods are superrich in vitamins, nutrients, and antioxidants and low in saturated fats. I'm talking about real food for helping you stay healthy, fit, and full of energy. Simply put, my Fantastic Fourteen are the best stuff you can give your body. Luckily, they taste so darn good it never feels like an obligation to find a place for them in my weekly menu. It's no surprise you'll find them throughout my book. Here's a quick primer on these foods and how they can help you give your body what it needs to keep in tip-top shape.

Avocado

We all need a moderate amount of fat in our diets, and an avocado is a great place to get it. You've probably heard it said before that avocado contains good fat. That's because most of the fat you find in an avocado is monounsaturated, which is a fancy way of saying it has heart-healthy fat. Add avocado to your next sandwich or salad and I guarantee it will make you feel more full and satisfied, which will help you make it to your next meal with less snacking in between.

Blueberries

I can't go past blueberries sprinkled over creamy desserts, baked into pies and cakes, or served simply with a dollop of low-fat Greek yogurt. Blueberries are high in antioxidants, which many nutritionists believe ward off inflammatory diseases and even cancer. And a great thing about blueberries is that their rich nutritional value gets locked in when they're frozen. So these humble berries can do your body good at any time of the year. Oh, and did I mention they're delicious?

Broccoli

If your mama is anything like mine, she's been telling you to eat your broccoli up since time began. That's because broccoli is one of the most vitamin-packed green vegetables you can feed your body. And I can't think of one kid who doesn't love it smothered in Cheddar cheese. I might skip the Cheddar more often than not these days, but I still mind my Mama's advice: Always finish your broccoli.

Eggs

Eggs tend to get a bad rap because of cholesterol, but you'd be surprised at how many health benefits are contained within their shells. Eggs are economical little packages of vitamins and nutrients. If you're watching your cholesterol, just cut down on the number of yolks you eat. But, if you're not, don't discount the yolks altogether, as they are loaded with protein. I like to use a mix of whole eggs and egg whites in most of my dishes.

Fat-Free or 2% Greek Yogurt

When I started watching my diet a little more closely, one of the first things I did was cut down on the amount of milk and cream I was consuming. But to get the calcium I needed for strong bones, I had to find a replacement. And that dairy replacement was fat-free or low-fat Greek yogurt. From savory to sweet to just plain on its own, this food has become a staple in my diet.

Fish

It really doesn't matter what fish you choose, from dark-meat salmon to white-meat grouper: We all need to eat more fish. Spending most of my time in the two coastal cities of Savannah and New York, it's easy for me to work a variety of fish into my diet whenever I want. If you don't live in a coastal city, however, it can be a bit more challenging. But I sure do recommend seeking out good fish. It's heart-healthy food because it contains the omega-3 fatty acid (with salmon being the best source). All fish really needs is a simple, quick preparation and dinner is on the table. And that adds up to the perfect midweek meal.

Lima Beans

Limas are a true superstar in the bean world. They are just so good for you it's ridiculous. These wonder beans are one of the best sources of fat-free fiber and protein there is. Why, eating limas can even help lower your cholesterol. They can be hard to find fresh, but frozen is a great way to go since they are snap frozen at picking, sealing in all the vitamin and mineral goodness that they have to offer. Southerners have understood the power of this little bean for a long time, and I think it's high time we shared the secret.

Nuts

Because nuts contain a fair amount of fat, I enjoy them in moderation. However, they add so much rich, layered flavor to a dish (not to mention protein, fiber, and magnesium). Keep an eye on portion control as you eat nuts, but don't cut them out of your diet. They are one of the most heart-healthy little snacks that nature has provided us.

Oats

Oatmeal is one of the most perfect pre-workout meals. It's loaded with good carbohydrates to fuel your muscles so that you can really maximize your workout. If you can, eat a bowl of oatmeal at least an hour before you work out to give you loads of energy without weighing you down.

Spinach

Spinach is so good for you that I'd need a whole other book to list all its benefits. It's a powerhouse of antioxidants, vitamins, and minerals. And, believe it or not, frozen spinach may just be better for you than fresh. You see, after spinach is picked, it immediately starts to lose nutritional value. As frozen spinach is snap frozen soon after picking, all that goodness is locked into the leaf, just waiting for you to unlock it when you reach for it in the freezer.

Sweet Potatoes

While I certainly do love white potatoes (particularly the French-fried variety), these days you're more likely to catch me enjoying a sweet potato. But it's not just because they are loaded with vitamins A and C. Mostly it's because they are such a tasty, sweet treat. Bake up a sweet potato and you'll see that you don't even need to dress it up with anything to make it shine.

Tofu

I find it's best to sneak tofu into dishes. When I mention it, the usual reaction is for people to wrinkle up their noses at me. But if I sneak it into a soup or stew without anyone knowing, I find diners eat it up like there's no tomorrow. I've even snuck it into some dishes I've served to Mama, without her ever being the wiser. But, let me tell you, you are wise if you find a way to use this low-fat, high-protein, iron-rich ingredient. For a great introduction to this somewhat exotic food, give my Secret Ingredient Butternut Squash Soup (page 25) a whirl.

Tomatoes

All I can say is, thank goodness tomatoes are good for you, because, if you're anything like me, they show up in almost every meal, whether it be dinner, lunch, or even breakfast. Packed with vitamins, beta-carotene, fiber, you name it and tomatoes have it. So don't be shy about working some into as many meals as possible. And here's the even better news: You'll still get all those vitamins even if you're using the canned variety. That means you can enjoy the benefits of tomatoes right on through the year.

Turkey

Turkey is one of the tastiest, least expensive, and most readily available ways to get your daily allotment of protein. And talk about versatile! This superlean meat can be used in place of chicken breast or ground beef in just about any recipe. And here's the kicker. Turkey is lower in fat than beef and chicken but actually boasts more protein per ounce than either meat.

Acknowledgments

FIRST OFF, A HUGE THANKS goes out to my biggest fan and best friend, my Mama. Your beautiful spirit inspires me each and every day.

Thank you to my co-author, Melissa Clark, and her tireless and talented team: Nancy Duran, Sarah Huck, and Karen Rush. Thanks to my literary agent, Janis Donnaud. Thanks to our nutritionists: Deborah Grayson and Allison Tannenbaum.

Many thanks to my editor, Pamela Cannon, and the entire Ballantine Books team. I think y'all are the best in the business.

Thanks to my wonderful food stylist, Libbie Summers, and my fantastic photographer, Ben Fink, for making my food look as good as it tastes.

To the gang at The Lady & Sons Restaurant, I love and appreciate y'all so much. My utter trust in you gives me the ability to get projects like this done. A giant thanks also to the whole crew at Paula Deen Enterprises, most especially Sarah Meighen.

And thank you to the companies that so kindly loaned us the use of their products to make this book more beautiful: Le Creuset, shopSCAD, Juliska, Symmetrical Pottery, and Counter Evolution.

A big, heartfelt thanks, as always, to my family—Dad, Jamie, Brooke, Jack and Matthew.

And last, but certainly not least, I want to thank my trainer, my therapist, my life coach, my dear friend: Sam Carter. Sam, you started me on the journey that inspired this book. Each and every day I learn more from you about how to be a better man, on the outside *as well as* the inside. You're one of the good ones, buddy, and I'm proud to count you as a friend.

Bobby Deen

Index

Page references in *italics* refer to illustrations.

About the Authors

Born in Georgia, BOBBY DEEN is the son of famous Food Network host and bestselling cookbook author Paula Deen, as well as the host of his own show, the Cooking Channel's *Not My Mama's Meals*. Bobby, along with his brother, Jamie, got his start in the food business in 1989 delivering sandwiches as part of his mother's business, The Bag Lady. The three Deens then joined forces to open a restaurant, The Lady & Sons, in Savannah. Bobby is a regular guest on *Today*, *Good Morning America*, *Rachael Ray*, and *The Dr. Oz Show*. He is a frequent guest on many Food Network shows, including *Paula's Home Cooking*.

Writer MELISSA CLARK's work appears in *The New York Times*, *Food & Wine*, *Martha Stewart*, and *Real Simple*. She has also collaborated on more than twenty cookbooks, one of which received both a James Beard Award and the Julia Child Cookbook Award in 2000.